ALCHEMY
OF THE SOUL

BLACK
STUDIES
& critical thinking
EDUCATION

R. Deborah Davis
Series Editor

Rochelle Brock and Richard Greggory Johnson III
Executive Editors

Vol. 74

The Black Studies and Critical Thinking series
is part of the Peter Lang Education list.
Every volume is peer reviewed and meets
the highest quality standards for content and production.

PETER LANG
New York • Bern • Frankfurt • Berlin
Brussels • Vienna • Oxford • Warsaw

Joyce Piert

ALCHEMY
OF THE SOUL

AN AFRICAN-CENTERED EDUCATION

PETER LANG
New York • Bern • Frankfurt • Berlin
Brussels • Vienna • Oxford • Warsaw

Library of Congress Cataloging-in-Publication Data
Piert, Joyce.
Alchemy of the soul: an African-centered education / Joyce Piert.
pages cm. — (Black Studies and Critical Thinking; v. 74)
Includes bibliographical references and index.
1. African Americans—Education. 2. African American students—Race identity.
3. Afrocentrism—Study and teaching—United States. 4. Afrocentrism—United States.
5. Discrimination in education—United States.
6. Ethnicity in children—United States. I. Title.
LC2731.P54 371.829'96073—dc23 2015008448
ISBN 978-1-4331-2699-4 (hardcover)
ISBN 978-1-4331-2698-7 (paperback)
ISBN 978-1-4539-1561-5 (e-book)
ISSN 1947-5985

Bibliographic information published by **Die Deutsche Nationalbibliothek**.
Die Deutsche Nationalbibliothek lists this publication in the "Deutsche
Nationalbibliografie"; detailed bibliographic data are available
on the Internet at http://dnb.d-nb.de/.

Cover design by Archie Walker

The paper in this book meets the guidelines for permanence and durability
of the Committee on Production Guidelines for Book Longevity
of the Council of Library Resources.

© 2015 Peter Lang Publishing, Inc., New York
29 Broadway, 18th floor, New York, NY 10006
www.peterlang.com

Printed in the United States of America

Dedicated to the Creator
who purposed me for this task and sustained me through it
And to the ancestors who have come before me and prepared the way
For such a time as this
Also to my father, Oscar Mitchell (1932–2000)
and
To my mother, Deolar Aubrey

TABLE OF CONTENTS

FOREWORD

However, I must prepare you for an intense lesson in understanding the historical perspectives of key African Americans...in this quest for an education that equips African Americans with the skills for self-determination...(p. 12)

This description, excerpted from the first chapter in this book, tells the reader—in part—what Joyce Piert sought to do in producing this extraordinary book. In this volume, she does a spectacular job of (a) defining African-centered education, (b) exploring the various "models of African-centeredness," and (c) describing the experiences of some of those who were involved in one African-centered school—turned charter school—in Michigan. But, more than that, she chronicles the development of African-centered education in this country and analyzes this important phenomenon with a critical eye.

An important organization involved in the effort to provide African-centered education for more than 40 years is the Council of Independent Black Institutions (CIBI).[1] In 1972, the CIBI, an umbrella organization for independent African-centered schools, was founded in Frogmore, South Carolina. Individuals at that historic meeting included Kasisi Jitu Weusi, John Churchville, Ndugu Lubengula, and others, representing 14 independent African-centered schools that were operating at that time. The founders had met with other Black educators earlier in the year to consider the current status of Black children's education. Two camps had developed from the earlier meeting. One group wanted to continue to pursue community control of schools. Weusi and his colleagues sought a second route: independent African-centered schools. During that founding meeting, Weusi was selected as the first chairman of CIBI.

Now in its 43rd year, CIBI promotes African-centered education nationally and internationally, in part through the sharing of information, materials, and curriculum. Member institutions seek to practice the Nguzo Saba, or the Seven Principles of Blackness, a value system developed by Dr. Maulana Karenga in the 1960s.[2] For CIBI, African-centeredness consists of the following:

- An acknowledgment of the essence of African spirituality (Ani, 1994; Anwisye, 1993; Clarke, 1991; Richards, 1980/1989).
- The practice of self-determination (Karenga, 1980).
- A focus on self-reliance, nation maintenance, and nation management (Clarke, 1991).
- Acknowledgment of the link between Black families and nationhood.
- An understanding of the relevance of African customs, traditions, rituals, and ceremonies.
- An emphasis on the link between African identity and African cultural history.
- A focus on knowledge and discovery of historical truths, through comparison, hypothesizing, testing, debate, trial and application, analysis and synthesis, creative and critical thinking, problem resolution processes, and final evaluation and decision making (Akoto, 1992).
- A conscious engagement in the process of Afrikan-centered personal transformation.
- Strict reliance on human perception and interpretation (Shujaa, 1992).
- An understanding that "children are the reward of life."[3]

In the mid-1990s, CIBI also addressed the issue of what it means for an educational institution to be independent. It concluded that independence has three components:

- A focus on nation building and obtaining land.
- A Pan African framework for decision making in pursuing, receiving, and investing funds.
- A community-based budget for essential expenses.

Since 1972, more than 150 African-centered educational institutions have been members of CIBI. Some current CIBI members have been operating since the 1970s, including NationHouse Watoto School in Washington, DC; Frederick Douglass Institute in St. Louis, Missouri; Roots Activity Learning Center in Washington, DC; New Concept Development Center in Chicago, Illinois; New World Learning Center in San Antonio, Texas; and Ujamaa Shule in Washington, DC (founded in 1968).

One former member of CIBI was Faizah Shule/Marcus Garvey Preparatory Academy (FS/MGPA),[4] a K–12 school founded in 1974 as an independent African-centered educational institution, later transitioning into a charter school that sought to practice aspects of African-centeredness. FS/MGPA operated for over 40 years, closing its doors in October 2013. This book is largely about the experiences of former students at FS/MGPA.

In this important volume, Piert begins by chronicling in creative and clear detail the impact of her upbringing on her deep commitment to Black people in general and Black education in particular. She recounts how she became devoted to understanding the nature of Black education and how she ultimately sought to relate the experiences of some former participants in an African-centered educational environment. She says in Chapter 1, "My life experiences with education both formal and informal nurtured the desire to create schools that would address the concerns of African American communities" (p. 11). Piert speaks, in effect, to the true role of education. She then provides an historical and analytical exploration of the concept and delineation of the key components of African-centered education (e.g., curriculum, pedagogy, and organizational formats). From there, she reports on a study that she conducted of the experiences of students in one African-centered school, turned charter school. Piert's fundamental query begins in Chapter 1, where she highlights the primary critical questions that drove her:

- What kind of education would truly center descendants of Africa within their own culture?
- What would be the benefits of that educational experience?
- Could those who have had that experience delineate the benefits, if any, of this experience? (p. 11)[5]

In her report, she provides a description of the methodology she employed. She delineates the setting, including the history, daily protocols and rituals, and curriculum. Piert then provides colorful and exacting descriptions of the respondents' voices—the students whom she interviewed.

Piert concludes that there were four student outcomes that were sought and in many cases achieved in FS/MGPA: a commitment to (a) nation building, (b) cultural knowledge, (c) self-advocacy, and (d) personhood. She describes the personal challenges that some of the students experienced as a result of attending an African-centered school. Interestingly, she also talks about the challenges faced by FS/MGPA as a result of its conversion from an African-centered school to a public charter school. Finally, Piert concludes with useful recommendations for the field and realistic suggestions for further research.

Piert has provided a thoughtful, honest, theoretical, and practical discussion of African-centered education. This work illuminates educational pedagogy in the context of an African-centered school. It is a refreshing and valuable read—particularly given the scarcity of high quality work on this topic.

Kofi Lomotey
Western Carolina University

Kofi Lomotey is the Bardo Distinguished Professor of Educational Leadership at Western Carolina University in Cullowhee, North Carolina. His publishing and research interests are in the areas of Black education, Black principals, and urban education. He served as the National Executive Officer of CIBI from 1976 through 1987.

ACKNOWLEDGMENTS

It helps to bring the spirits of other people into your life. It gives you many more eyes to see and helps overcome limitations.

—*Sobonfu Somé* (1999)

I give praise to the Creator for the journey that has brought me to this book and I acknowledge the ancestors who have prepared the way before me for this task. I acknowledge the Spirits of African people throughout the diaspora.

My deepest gratitude goes to members of the I AM Institute for Learning LLC (IAMIL), who endured my frustrations and gently loved and supported me until the book was complete. I give special thanks to Charles Xzavier Simon; the twins, Aubrey and Archie Walker; NeoGenesis (Benjamin Johnson); my niece, Isis (Brittany Mitchell), and so many more, who challenged me into inspiration. It was through their insights that I was able to write in a new way, the way of spirit, vibration, and frequency. I especially want to thank all those who took time to read my "long" manuscript and lovingly provided suggestions that made this book so much better. Special thanks to my longtime friend, Kefentse Chike, who came into my life to stretch and challenge my thinking around the topic of this book.

I extend special gratitude to my mother, Deolar Aubrey, for being a vessel used by the Creator to nurture and love me into my purpose. I am indebted to my children, Shahied and Rashida Aquil, for their support. I am also grateful in advance to my nieces and nephews who will accept the baton to continue the race toward the liberation of African people everywhere, essentially the liberation of humanity!

The creative genius for my book cover design is attributed to a good friend (aforementioned in this acknowledgment) but deserving of another shout out…Archie Walker. Archie is the CEO and founder of the The Arch Aspect. He is a talented hands-on graphic designer. Archie's versatility focuses on creating everything from company branding and advertising to shooting music videos. Archie is highly sought after for his brilliant creations and can be contacted at archie@thearchaspect.com.

LIST OF ADINKRA SYMBOLS

In this book, I chose to put selected Adinkra symbols in front of the titles. I believe that these symbols permitted me to add additional meaning to each chapter through their representation. The symbols are part of a long-standing symbolic language of the Ghanaian people and were historically used to transmit traditional values of the Asante/Akan people (Williams, 2011). In fact, these symbols can now be found globally in textiles, art, and media (Agbo, 1999; Williams, 2011). I chose to incorporate these symbols to introduce each chapter. My intent was to provide a visual image, which I believe is undergirded with an ancestral energy that imparts a vibrational message to the reader. Essentially, as the reader perceives the Adinkra symbol, a spiritual impartation will prepare the reader for the next journey through the book.

ADINKRA SYMBOL	MEANING IN TWI	ENGLISH TRANSLATION
	MMERE DANE	"Time changes"
	FAWAHODIE	"Independence comes with its responsibilities"
	NEA ONNIM NO SUA A, OHU	"He who does not know can know from learning"
	ONYANKOPON ADOM NTI BIRIBIARA BEYE YIE	"By God's grace all will be well"
	MMUSUYIDEE	"That which removes bad luck"
	SESA WO SUBAN	"I change or transform my life"
	ODO NNYEW FIE KWAN	"Love never loses its way home"
	NYAME NTI	"By God's grace"
	SANKOFA	"Return and get it"
	NYAME YE OHENE	"God is King"

Adinkra Symbols: Adinkra symbols and meanings from a free source website: http://www.adinkra. org/index.htm

1.   THE DREAM WITHIN A DREAM

And dreams are the language of God. When he speaks in our language, I can interpret what he has said. But if he speaks in the language of the soul, it is only you who can understand. (Coelho & Clarke, 1988/1993, p. 9)

The Dream

The children were lined up in a long row, and they ranged in age from 3 to 5. They were young and diverse in race, but the file of children was mostly composed of children of color. They looked ahead, almost like robots, not given to distractions as most young people their age, but intensely focused on keeping in step with the child in front. I was leading the group like a Pied Piper of sorts, being careful not to walk too swiftly, ever conscious of the young stride that followed me in lockstep. We were walking down a street. It was the business section of a town and it appeared to be one of the busiest streets that could exist in any town. In fact, cars were careening past us on the right, while lines of buildings were stretching to the sky on the left. We were sandwiched between these two impenetrable forces. As I looked ahead, I could see that we were approaching a clearing. The long fortress of buildings was ending as if cut off like an unexpected cliff and an intersection of streets emerged. I could now see cars sitting patiently waiting for the light at the intersection to change to green, giving them permission to leave the gate like horses at a race waiting for the sound of gunfire to signal the beginning of the race. But they were stopped at the light, eager to move forward but constrained. So, as I walked to the intersection, I quickly scanned the long line of children behind me. They reminded me of a long tail dragging behind me like Puff the magic dragon. I smiled to myself as I thought of their innocence and my heart warmed. I thought about how much these young beings trusted me to guide them down this long dangerous street and I felt so blessed. I was their teacher and their parents confidently shared their most precious gifts, their children, with me. "Wow!" I thought to myself, what an awesome task to undertake, to lead the children. As I relished these thoughts in my mind, I realized that I was now well into the intersection and the children were keeping with my step, moving swiftly and with great fluidity, but the intersection was wide and we were only a fourth of the way across when the light suddenly changed. "Oh my God! I thought as I frantically considered how to get the children out of the streets and onto the sidewalk on the other side. The cars were now moving across the intersection in front of me, although the cars behind me were sitting, waiting patiently as my children were passing through, but we had a long way to go and more children were entering into the roadway as we walked. The line was so long, so long! How am I going to do this and keep my children safe?" I thought. Now the children in the front with me could feel my concern and they began to become distracted. They started looking at the cars around them rather than at me. I could feel the dis-ease begin to move through my line of children like a virus, and like a domino effect manifesting before my eyes, disruption ignited and the unthinkable happened. One child, who must have been the most attuned to my concern, broke from the lockstep of the cadence in the line. This beautiful being, who a second ago had been diligently moving forward, became a traitor to the group, and in his own attempt to find a solution to the growing dissonance of the group, he shifted the movement of the group. Very smoothly, but within a second, that child shifted his body away from the direction of the group and then unlocked his foot from the lockstep in one seamless motion and began to take action. He began to sprint with legs stretching forward and arms whipping like a turbine engine. He had one goal in mind and that was to get to the other side of the intersection as quickly as possible. In that moment he committed mutiny and blindly led his herd of compliant rebels out into the oncoming traffic. Right before my eyes in that space where no amount of my shouting to remain calm could drown out the screeching of tires, the yelling of children, the cracking of bones, and slamming on brakes, I found myself in slow motion, observing the chaotic scene of little bodies soaring through the air as if they had grown wings like the little angels that they were. Fear and pain congealed as one huge lump in my throat, choking out my own voice. I closed my eyes as if removing that scene from my eyes would allow me to erase it from my reality. But surprisingly, it appeared to work, the noise stopped abruptly! Instant silence filled my ears! I opened my eyes and it was then that I realized that I had been dreaming. It was all just a dream, a horrible dream! I had been dreaming.

As I lay in my bed pondering the significance of this dream, I realized that the universe was telling me something significant. It was a clear message, challenging for me to receive at first but necessary for me to hear. I heard a voice in my head say, "You're not ready yet!" Now, I looked around in the darkness of the room and felt for a presence. I became focused and tuned my ears to hear the slightest motion. Nothing moved and I could only hear the pounding of my own heart. "Hmm," I thought. "I must be hearing things!" Almost immediately, as if to dispel any comfort in rationalizations, the voice spoke again: "You're not ready yet! You will hurt the children!" As a captive listener, how do I run from that? How do I offer any defense to that?

What does this mean, that "I will hurt the children"? I love the children. I only want to assist the children in reaching their unlimited potential as human beings, or so I thought. I am a mature African American woman, considered by the younger ones to be an elder in the educational community. I have instructed a myriad of students in urban and suburban educational institutions, in both secondary and postsecondary environments. The identity of a teacher is a welcome one to me. I wear it like a bonnet on Easter Sunday in any Baptist Church in my community. Head held high and strutting my stuff, so to speak, I felt a joy to be able to impact other beings. So, I knew that this message did not address my heart's love for them, but rather I believed that it addressed my discernment of this nation's educational system's complexities and the consequences resulting from them.

However, I was reluctant to admit that the source of this communication knew more about me than I did. This uncertainly about my knowledge of self ignited a desire to know more, at least to know what the voice seemed certain to know, and this fueled a passion to deconstruct this dream and find the answers to questions brewing in my mind.

As I began this process of deconstruction, I was reminded of a similar journey of the character Santiago in Coelho and Clarke's (1988/1993) book, *The Alchemist*. The Andalusian shepherd boy, Santiago, sets out on a quest to find a treasure that he is told about in a dream. In his sojourn, he encounters significant people, places, and situations that present life lessons, and his efforts to find this treasure reveal a vast amount of information about him. His inescapable self-expansion eventually changes his perspective on where the true treasure is located and he accepts the necessity of this journey in preparation for the possession of this coveted treasure. Likewise for me, my dream was the catalyst that would cause me to discover treasures in unique and unexpected places. However, I must begin to step out in this discovery, even as Santiago stepped out in his pursuit.

The term *dream* has several definitions. A dream can be "a series of thoughts, visions, or feelings that happen during sleep," or it can be "an idea or vision that is created in your imagination and that is not real" (Dream, n.d.). The dream began with my dream. It may not seem clear as I have shared it, but the dream implicated my life's dream: the dream of leading children by starting my own school. Early in my life, I decided that I wanted to create, develop, and operate a school that would liberate the minds and hearts of people of African descent, although I would later come to understand that all people emerged from Africa. Since this dream has led me to ponder my dream, I want to share how my dream (life's purpose) was developed throughout my life, for a better understanding of how this dream speaks to me.

> It's the possibility of having a dream come true that makes life interesting, he thought. (Coelho & Clarke, 1988/1993, p. 8)

The Dream Within a Dream

My story begins with the early development of a sense of community, cultural awareness, and spirituality. Traditionally, the adults in African communities were the transmitters of community traditions, values, and roles for the young children in the village (Tedla, 1995). Reflecting back over my early years, I must admit that I was submerged in a community of adults who were able to transcend the drama of life in America and without deliberate effort were able to model agency and activism. While incubated in this environment, I was able to dream a dream of purpose.

In America, the Great Migration of the 1940s and 1950s was a significant time, when huge numbers of African Americans left the agricultural terrain of the South and headed to the industrial centers of the Northeast and Midwest. African Americans began to occupy urban spaces, and as a response to racism and discrimination, they developed small African American economic strips within these spaces. These decades were followed by the turbulent 1960s, a decade full of unrest and civil disobedience as this nation wrestled with issues of racism, social justice, and inequality.

The 1960s was a time when African American communities were still primarily segregated in enclaves located within urban areas. It was a time when families still gathered on the porch in late evenings and told stories of the day's events. Oftentimes, when major crises were in the forefront of the news, these porches became the judge and jury, including weighing the evidence and declaring a verdict, even before formal proceedings commenced. I remember, as a child, sitting through one of these informal trial court discussions one Saturday, where neighbors were deliberating over who was the most effective civil rights activist, Martin Luther King Jr. or Malcolm X. It was a discussion that lasted from early afternoon to late night on that porch, where the participants weaved in and out as folks left and returned. Three times, Mrs. Jones sent their son, Terry, down to the porch to get Mr. Jones for dinner. Mr. Dunbar showed up halfway through this gathering and took to pontificating as if he had been there all along. You could hear them up and down the streets; in fact, other folks on the block started having their own discussions. The community was lit up that day over the validity of Martin or Malcolm in the freedom of Black folks.

I grew up experiencing community as this place in which children learn their roles in society. The microcosm of my society was filtered through the lens of a color conscious world. As I watched *The Donna Reed Show* or *Father Knows Best*, I became aware that my "community" experienced a different reality. In my young mind, I was not able to clearly decipher how this vast difference in social experience was created. I knew that my mother did not move about the kitchen in a meticulously painted face, high heels, and an apron, and dad did not come home wearing a suit and tie to a prepared hot meal. In fact, my mother was struggling to bring variety to oatmeal, which my two brothers and I ate for breakfast, lunch, and dinner, because our alcoholic father was gambling his money away in the basement with his dad and brothers.

My father's family packed up in the 1950s, leaving Arkansas and journeying north to pursue a better life. My dad, his father, and his younger brother gladly left lumber mill jobs behind in an effort to acquire factory jobs in the automotive industry in the city of Flint, Michigan. They were seduced by the hope of earning wages that would allow them to achieve the promised "American Dream" of this nation. However, it became routine that on most Fridays, which were paydays, it was a throw of the dice, literally, if my dad's money made it home to take care of necessities. My family survived. We survived through the big heart of community and the fact that the sense of community went beyond our own household. Everyone in our community were considered family, and if you needed sugar, your neighbor gave you sugar; if you needed bread, then your neighbors shared their bread but they also shared their counsel and love. As I grew up, I came to understand the value of community by the behaviors that were modeled for me.

When I reflect back, I also realize that it was through that same community that activism and self-efficacy were modeled. At those community porch gatherings, I learned the love and respect for the values of freedom, justice, and equality for all people. It seemed that every day I was able to interact with someone in the community who was actively engaged in decrying discrimination and the injustices perpetrated on African Americans around the nation.

Most notably, I now realize that in prepuberty, I was groomed in the struggle for social justice for African American people. My father's cousin, Sam, would often come and visit with him. This was always a natural occurrence, since my father's parents lived next door and Sam would visit with his aunt and uncle occasionally. During those visits to the house, random discussions would ensue around recent events of racism. On one particular visit, Uncle Sam, which is ironically what I called him, began speaking passionately about this new organization that he had joined. He shared his perspectives on how the Nation of Islam (NOI) was going to liberate the Black man in America.

This uncle just happened to be my favorite, and he would always tickle me to make me laugh. I idolized him because he seemed to be so smart, and on this particular visit, he began to say things that I had never heard but intrigued me. He told my father that this man, Elijah Muhammad, was the leader of the NOI and the messenger from Allah. He shared that Muhammad was going to set Black people free and create a nation for them. He said that the Black man was the original man and that the White man was the devil. In all the conversations that I had been made privy to on those neighborhood porches, I had never heard that. Yes, I paid attention as I observed those conversations, although the traditions of our community would not tolerate me to blurt out any comments without experiencing consternation or a stern rebuke. I knew all too well that something was wrong with the structure of this world that I was in. I knew that it was unfair that some people had advantages because of the color of their skin, while others were penalized for their complexions. I also understood that I happened to be in the group that seemed to be penalized for a condition that was beyond its control.

The anger that Uncle Sam's statements invoked in my father brought me to full attention. My father is normally an easygoing and fun-loving person. He assumed a perspective of mild acceptance when considering the injustices that were occurring daily; he would mumble under his breath, "This is just the way it is." But Uncle Sam's attempts to champion this organization to my father were met with a harsh rebuke. My father was not having it! However, Uncle Sam was like a used car salesman who felt that he was just about to make that closing deal, and so he invited my father to accompany him to the next service at the Muhammad Mosque No. 53. Quite as I had expected, my father declined the offer. But I was totally unprepared for what happened next, and it caught everyone in the room off guard. My mother, who is normally nonintrusive in these conversations, spoke up from her quiet corner of the room and told my uncle that she was interested in going with him to the next meeting. At that moment, I felt such delight, while my father's mouth fell open! I knew that my mother must have heard my insides shouting and screaming to attend that meeting. I wanted to go and I needed one of my parents to be my entrance into that world. I knew that convincing my mother would be so much easier than trying to plead with my father to let me accompany him. I just knew, even at such a young age, that this was something that my soul ached to experience.

So at the age of 12, I became a member of the NOI. My membership into this organization was initiated with a letter addressed to Messenger Elijah Muhammad sent to the headquarters in Chicago and signed by my mother. I received a letter a few weeks later confirming that I was now a Black Muslim and belonged to the Muslim Girls Training (MGT).

Although the NOI was founded by Fard Muhammad in 1934 (Salaam, 2013), by the time I joined, it was under the leadership of Elijah Muhammad. The NOI was an African American organization perceived by European Americans as threatening and militant, while perceived by African Americans as Black Nationalist and self-determining. The NOI was a community of African Americans who promoted the ideology of self-reliance and independence for African Americans and Africans.

It was here in this community of the NOI that I was nurtured in a value system of Black Nationalism, which espoused racial solidarity, self-determination, and self-sufficiency of African peoples in the world. In my home environment and community, I was well aware that I was a "Black" person, but being Black seemed to have very few benefits. Yes, I could enjoy the music of people who were my color and even dance with "rhythm," but the tangible benefits of Blackness were negated or simply omitted as I viewed the voices of the dominant media. Blackness meant that my skin wasn't light enough, my hair wasn't straight enough, my nose wasn't pointed enough, or I just wasn't smart enough. It was in the environment created by the NOI that I was first introduced to authentic "self-love."

Self-love began when I learned that my identity as an African American had so many undisclosed benefits. I immediately learned that as a descendant of African people, my ancestors existed long before the slave trade began. I learned that African people were the first to populate the Earth and that all others originated from these dark-skinned people. I learned that family and community were primary to the building of a nation and that African and

African American people needed to strengthen their family unit in order to strengthen their nations. It was in this environment that I learned that as a woman of African descent, my role in the uplift of the Black race was essential to the renaissance of the family. In the MGT and General Civilization classes I attended on Saturday mornings, I was instructed in the fundamental skills and knowledge for maintaining a family, parenting, and strategies for minimizing the impact of the oppressive elements of the dominant culture on Black children.

The Fruit of Islam, also known as the FOI, was the training structure of the NOI for men and operated as the security force for the organization. The men were called *fruit* because the term was symbolic of the central role of the Black man in creating the new nation. As a young person growing up in this environment, I idolized the FOI for several reasons. For one, many of these men had been incarcerated or were substance abusers. The NOI was able to take these men, often recruiting them while incarcerated or pulling them out of drug dens, and "cleaned" them up. My young heart would beam in love and admiration as I watched rows and rows of Black men marching in unison, like a well-choreographed dance. These men donned blue uniforms, white shirts with blue bow ties, and shining black shoes. In that sea of sober faces, none cracked a smile and all looked straight ahead in a collective focus. My self-love was further enhanced as I saw people who looked like me in positions of power, such as captains, lieutenants, squad leaders, ministers, assistant ministers, and such (Salaam, 2013). In this community, I learned that power was not determined by monetary capital but rather by a circle of influence to improve the condition of Black people. This was certainly contrary to the messages that I was receiving from the media regarding Black people.

My Black consciousness grew in this robust environment, along with my awareness of the massive inequalities that were affecting people of color in this nation and globally. There were always standing discussions on the struggles of African nations as they sought independence from their European colonizers. Independence and a separate nation was the mantra of that time for the NOI. Consequently, the Black Muslims operated independent schools and businesses in African American communities throughout the United States. I learned to see the world from a position of empowerment, agency, and efficacy rather than victimization and lack. I was encouraged and guided in the reclamation of my cultural heritage.

When Elijah Muhammad purchased Temple No. 1 in Chicago, I was thrilled and full of pride. The annual visit to Chicago on Savior's Day would mean enduring long lines of women clad in white from head to toe. The lines were so long that it would take several hours to be patted down for security purposes and then led to a seat. After hearing Elijah Muhammad give the Savior's Day address, we would hurriedly travel down the road to have dinner in the exquisite Muslim-owned restaurant. I remember that there was a fountain of juice in the middle of the restaurant in which customers would hold their glass under the perpetually flowing spigots and get as much of the healthy fruit juice as their cup could hold. At the bakery down the street, I was tantalized by the taste of "bean" pies and "bean" ice cream. Muhammad encouraged his members to eat healthily, highlighting the health benefits of eating legumes; thus beans were incorporated into desserts. I also remember walking up and down streets full of Muslim-owned businesses, such as bakeries, restaurants, newspapers, publishers, a grocery store, shoe stores, clothing stores, and much more. Muslims were encouraged to "do for self."

Spiritually, I experienced an ideological shift from the Christian religious perspective of my immediate family to the "Islamic" perspective of the Black Muslims. I must say that now, I well understand that this was a diluted version of traditional Orthodox Islam and was strategically presented this way by Fard Muhammad (Rashid & Muhammad, 1992). In the NOI, Christianity was perceived as the "White man's religion," which taught African Americans to believe that their God was "White" and looked like Michelangelo's cousin, in other words, like a "long-haired White man with blues eyes, thin lips, and a pointed nose." I gladly adopted the concept that my God would look like me, with a Black face and woolly hair.

The NOI opened independent University of Islam schools around the nation. The schools were created as a means to inculcate children of the members in African cultural values and norms, which promoted the liberation of Africans in America and in the diaspora. In fact, at the age of 17, I became a teacher in one of these schools in central Michigan. At that time, I was under the mentorship of the school director, Bro. Nathaniel X, who had been a teacher in the traditional public school system. Through Bro. Nathaniel X, I was able to meld everything that I was learning together and provide academic instruction while modeling the cultural norms and values that I had acquired. Under his tutelage, I was able to birth forth my love for teaching, and I learned to engage my heart in the symbiosis of the instructional process. I was keenly aware that my students and their parents belonged to my family, this extended family that was created in the organization. Although we did not refer to each other as "mama" or "baba," the elders were given the upmost respect and everyone was protective of each other. In fact, the FOI, which was the military arm of the organization, would be known to "right" any wrong committed against its members. I understood that teaching the children about their culture and heritage was critical to the uplift of African people and their descendants everywhere.

Although I had the experience of cultural reclamation during my youth, years later I found myself without the resources to provide this "African-centered" type of education for my own children. In fact, the struggle to get my own two children through the American public school system was the vehicle that moved me toward the research that is the focus of this book. My son remained in high school for five years instead of the traditional four, in order to graduate, while my daughter dropped out of school in the 11th grade, eventually completing a GED from an alternative high school. Our situation was contrary to research that asserts that the parents' attitudes toward education and the family's socioeconomic status impact the student's academic success; my children were raised in a middle-class home environment (Ansalone, 2009). Both their father and I were attending college during their childhood and adolescent years. Education was promoted as the key to success, and our cultural values within the home were closely aligned with the middle-class values of the school. Cultural pride was primacy in our home environment and our children were aware of their African heritage. Yet I could not convince my children that the education they were receiving in the public schools was valuable to their future. They were rejecting the education of the public schools, and only through our unrelenting nagging and haranguing did they acquiesce to complete the process, culminating in graduation. I was distraught and assumed that my children's difficulties were attributed to some deficiency in their home environment; however, when I looked around, I found so many of my African American neighbors, friends, and relatives in the same predicament with their children. What was going on? Why didn't these young people see the value in education?

These challenges were the catalyst that fueled my desire to pursue a degree in the field of education. While pursuing my undergraduate degree, a friend and I developed and coordinated a four-week summer program for urban children in Grades 5 through 12. This program offered courses in language arts, mathematics, and African American history. We were able to secure volunteer teachers for the program from the local university. Our program continued for five years. Student enrollment progressed from approximately 50 students to over 100 and had a waiting list by the fifth year. We discovered that our students responded positively to the smaller class size, caring teachers, and instruction in African American history from an African-centered perspective. Many of our students demonstrated the impact that this experience had on them by becoming honor roll students when they returned to public school. These students' testimonials praised the genuine care and faith of the instructors in the students and their abilities to succeed in the learning environment.

My life experiences with education, both formal and informal, nurtured the desire to create schools that would address the concerns of African American communities. Specifically, my childhood experiences were painted with broad strokes by the fallout from the racialization of dark-skinned people in this nation. I lived during the time of a seething and escalating eruption of a long-suffering and wearied people who were now demanding equality for all people in this reluctant nation. These experiences were vital and led to the sculpting and development of my ideology around education for African American children. The challenges that I experienced with my children's journey through the educational process in the traditional public schools, along with the positive impact and motivation that my summer program had on the lives of other children, translated into desire. These experiences acted as the catalyst to be instrumental in providing African American students the educational experience that would display respect to their culture and their humanity.

With this desire in my heart, I began a journey of gathering information. I wanted to understand how to create an educational experience that would impact the lives of young people in a positive manner. Questions arose in my mind demanding consideration: What kind of education would truly center descendants of Africa within their own culture? What would be the benefits of that educational experience? Could those who have had that experience delineate the benefits, if any, of this experience?

These questions were poised in my mind when I entered the doctoral program at Michigan State University, focusing on educational administration with a K–12 specialization. When it was time to declare my research question, I never wavered: "What is the best education for African American children?" The chairperson of my guidance committee said, "Joyce, that may be a bit too broad for a topic; let's narrow that down a bit." With his prodding me forward and incessant in-depth probing of new questions that I offered, along with numerous renditions of questions, we were able to narrow the research question to something manageable: "What are the experiences of African American young people who attend an African-centered school?"

Now that I had the question in hand, I knew that I was on my way to discovering the answer to my dream, which was still puzzling to me. As I reflect
over my life, I can see that there were situations and circumstances that were
guiding me to undertake this research. My early exposure to the NOI and
Black Nationalism birthed in me the ideology of self-determination and set
me on this course of discovery. Was it fate that led me to this task of mining
the literature fields seeking the origins of the African-centered educational
movement in this country? Or was it the universe aligning the pieces of my
story as I moved forward toward my dream, my treasure? It had to be that my
destination was being shaped by my dream; there was surely no way that I
could successfully develop education that would address the needs of African
Americans without understanding how education was pursued throughout
their involuntary sojourn here in these United States. Of course, it was the
dream that caused me to take the first step to posing the question.

As I dissected the literature, I found that African societies had always pursued education for their members (Mbiti, 1970; Menkiti, 1984; Tedla, 1995).
Education was not a formal practice as we experience it today; it was informal and infused with the life experience of community and society. In many
African societies, children learned as apprentices under adult tutelage. Yet
education happened! More specifically, early in the history of Africans here in
America, education occurred, and the desire to expropriate it led to what we
currently identify as the African-centered educational model.

In the following chapter, I share the path of determined purpose that led
to this educational model in America. However, I must prepare you for an
intense lesson in understanding the historical perspectives of key African
Americans that I have identified in this quest for an education that equips
African Americans with the skills for self-determination. I have only identified the ones that I felt were substantial in the movement, but I must con-
fess that my list is not exhaustive. You will also acquire a comprehensive
knowledge of the African-centered educational model as defined by noted
Afrocentrists and scholars.

2. ROOTS OF AN AFRICAN-CENTERED EDUCATIONAL MODEL

As he mused about these things, he realized that he had to choose between thinking of himself
as the poor victim of a thief and as an adventurer in quest of his treasure. (Coelho & Clarke,
1988/1993, p. 30)

The African-centered educational movement in the United States was due
to the collective and self-determined efforts of Africans in America, both free
and enslaved, to provide education for themselves and their children. This educational model, which existed in a rough evolving structure in the 17th and
18th centuries, was perceived as a necessary component in the drive toward
liberation, freedom, and independence of Africans in America. I discovered
that it is the consensus of current research on African-centered education
that this movement has its roots in Black Nationalism and Pan-Africanism
(Akoto, 1992; Asante, 1991; Essien-Udom, 1962; Ginwright, 2004).

One theorist, E. U. Essien-Udom (1962), defined Black Nationalism as
the following:

The belief of a group that it shares, or ought to share, a common heritage of language,
culture and religion; and that its heritage, way of life and ethnic identity are distinct
from those of other groups...that they ought to rule themselves and shape their own
destinies. (p. 20)

The Black Nationalist movement is integral to Pan-Africanism. Pan-Africanism is the belief that Africans on the African continent and in the diaspora should unite against European colonialism and White supremacy (Moses, 1978). As I explored further, I found that these ideologies were the philosophical guides that drove the African-centered educational movement.

Essien-Udom (1962), Moses (1978), and Redkey (1969) have documented the genesis of the Black Nationalist and Pan-Africanist ideology with Paul Cuffe, a free-born African in America in 1815. Despite being a free African ship owner in New Bedford, Massachusetts, Cuffe had become disillusioned with America's hypocrisy in keeping Africans enslaved while ringing the bells for their own liberation from England. He founded the Friendly Society for the Emigration of Free Negroes from America, and using his personal funds, took 38 African Americans to Sierra Leone (Clarke, 1994).

Martin R. Delany, also a Black Nationalist and Pan-Africanist during the mid-19th century, championed the establishment of a state by African Americans in the Niger Valley. In fact, he was instrumental in negotiating an agreement with several African kings for this project (Clarke, 1994). During the late 19th and early 20th centuries, there were other African Americans who articulated the Black Nationalist and Pan-African ideologies, such as Bishop Henry McNeal Turner, Alexander Crummell, and W. E. B. Du Bois.

However, the most influential proponent of the Black Nationalist and Pan-African movements was Marcus Garvey, who, through the Universal Negro Improvement Association (UNIA), advocated self-determination and the economic, social, and political uplift of African people in America and in the diaspora. He preached the "confraternity of the Brotherhood" between all Africans. Garvey also espoused the reclamation of Africa, which was established in this chant of UNIA members: "Africa for the Africans, those at home and those abroad" (Maglangbayan, 1972, p. 21).

After Garvey was deported by the federal government for what some now declare as fraudulent charges of mail fraud, Elijah Muhammad inherited Black Nationalism and Pan-Africanism from the Garveyites (Ginwright, 2004). Muhammad advocated separate schools and a separate nation for African Americans within America. Like Garvey, Muhammad was a proponent of African Americans educating their own and establishing their own financial base. As Muhammad was organizing African Americans toward self-determination and agency, national unrest gave rise to the Black Power and Civil Rights movements.

The 1960s were wrought with racial and civil unrest, which was manifested in various degrees of protest through sit-ins, boycotts, marches, and riots. Early in this decade, the Black Power ideology, which espoused racial pride and group solidarity, began to spread throughout the African American communities as a result of the struggle against America's racist and oppressive social structure. Karenga (1988) referred to this decade as the period in which people of African descent made the "most severe and successful theoretical and practical criticism of the structure and content of U.S. society" (p. 125). Ginwright (2004) posited that Black Nationalism and Pan-Africanism undergirded the ideology of the Black Power movement, which placed Africa as the nexus of the political and cultural agenda for African Americans.

In the midst of the Black Power movement, students on major college and university campuses across the nation were critiquing these institutions of learning as microcosms of the larger racist society (Karenga, 1988). Students, both African American and European American, believed that these educational institutions promoted racism through the exploitation and oppression of people of color. Karenga (1988) contended that this exploitation of people of color was accomplished by their purposeful exclusion from knowledge, wealth, and power. Subsequently, African American students on college and university campuses began to demand the establishment of Black Studies departments that offered courses expounding the Black experience. They "charged that traditional disciplines had not given attention to Black intellectual experience, culture, and history" (Okafor, 1996, p. 693). As a result of this student protest, Black Studies departments were instituted in major universities across the nation.

As the rally for Black Studies intensified, a young scholar emerged who became an instrument for furthering the African-centered education movement by providing a theoretical framework. Molefi K. Asante, while working as a director for the Center for Afro-American Studies at UCLA in the late 1960s, began formulating his thoughts for his insightful work, published in 1988: *Afrocentricity: The Theory of Social Change* (Asante, 1988/2003). *Afrocentricity* is a theoretical perspective of "resistance and agency" (Robinson, 2004, p. 104) and is a term that is often used interchangeably with *African centered, Afrocentric,* and *Africentricity*.

The ideologies of Black Nationalism (i.e., the belief that Africans share a common historical and cultural experience, and they should seek to determine their own destiny as a nation, race, and people distinct from others), Pan-Africanism (i.e., the belief that Africans on the continent and in the diaspora should unite against colonialism and White supremacy), and Black power (i.e., the belief that Africans on the continent and in the diaspora should be able to achieve self-determination, self-sufficiency, self-respect, and self-defense through the power that they possess) contributed to the theory of Afrocentricity. Asante (1988/2003) adroitly explicated Afrocentricity as the following:

> [A] mode of thought and action in which the centrality of African interests, values, and perspectives predominate. In regards to theory, it is the placing of African people in the center of any analysis of African phenomena. Thus, it is possible for anyone to master the discipline of seeking the location of Africans in a given phenomenon. In terms of action and behavior, it is a devotion to the idea that what is in the best interest of African consciousness is at the heart of ethical behavior. Finally, Afrocentricity seeks to enshrine the idea that blackness itself is a trope of ethics. Thus, to be black is to be against all forms of oppression, racism, classism, homophobia, patriarchy, child abuse, pedophilia, and white racial domination. (p. 2)

Contrary to critics' arguments, Afrocentricity is not an attempt by African American supremacists, separatists, or nationalists to impose an African worldview on others (Ravitch, 1990; Schlesinger, 1992). Asante (1991) debunked the critics by confirming that the theory of Afrocentricity does not promote a position of superiority in which it disaffirms other groups' perspectives but offers an alternative way of viewing phenomena. He posited that Afrocentricity theoretically challenges the Eurocentric perspective in three ways:

> First, it questions the imposition of the White supremacist view as universal and/or classical. Second, it demonstrates the indefensibility of racist theories that assault multiculturalism and pluralism. Finally, it projects a humanistic and pluralistic viewpoint by articulating Afrocentricity as a valid, nonhegemonic perspective. (Asante, 1991, p. 173)

Theorists of Afrocentricity applied the concept to the institutions of education and insisted that an education for African American children should reflect this ideology. These theorists further suggested that an African-centered educational model would be the most appropriate educational model for children of color, specifically African American children (Akoto, 1992; Asante, 1991; Lee, 1992; Shujaa, 1992). However, this educational model could not just be a superficial overlay of "Black" facts on a traditional curriculum. These theorists adamantly maintained that this educational model be the result of an African-centered curriculum, delivered utilizing African-centered pedagogy (Akoto, 1992; Asante, 1991; Lee, 1992).

This literature leads me to the conjecture that African-centered education was birthed forth out of a need for Africans in America to gain control over the directions of their lives. There was no human satisfaction in accepting the concept that "fate" had decided to enslave Africans and that second-class citizenship was just a natural consequence. In fact, it is beyond reason to decide that there was a benign acquiescence to this state of existence because the heavens had decreed it as so. As the old man had warned the boy, believing that our lives are controlled by fate is the world's greatest lie, and the historical account speaks clearly to Africans in America and their determination to create a reality that would allow self-efficacy and the celebration of their humanity (Coelho & Clarke, 1988/1993).

Yes, for African Americans, education was perceived as the key to controlling their destiny. This belief also guided my life's path. However, as my story illustrates, I was acquainted with this concept of an African-centered educational model when I was affiliated with the NOI. Although it was not referred to as African-centered education, it was an educational model established upon the culture and traditions of African American people. This educational model was loosely hung on the African-centered paradigm. In reality, it was simply a "Black face" rendition of the traditional White nationalist educational model offered in traditional public schools. It became apparent to me that I was missing a precise understanding of what this African-centered educational model looked like. Was it simply a "Black-faced" educational experience mimicking traditional public school, or should it be an educational model that reflected the values of Afrocentricity as posited by the theorists? This question ignited a yearning to examine the African-centered educational model. Was it a curriculum? Was it pedagogy? Or were African-centered curriculum and pedagogy necessary to achieve a quality education for African American students?

3. DEFINING AN AFRICAN-CENTERED
EDUCATIONAL MODEL

Don't forget that everything you deal with is only one thing and nothing else. And don't forget the language of omens. And, above all, don't forget to follow your destiny through to its conclusion. (Coelho & Clarke, 1988/1993, p. 22)

I now understood that the desire for self-determination through educational access was forefront in the minds of African American leaders at various historical junctures within American history. I knew that my destiny was leading me to discover how this educational model is defined by asking and answering the following questions: What are the components of this African-centered educational model and how are the components defined?

What Is an African-Centered Curriculum?

An African-centered curriculum is a guideline for the delivery of African-centered instruction. One prominent characteristic of an African-centered curriculum is that it is established on the theory of *Afrocentricity*. Although Asante (1988/2003) was credited with formalizing the concept of Afrocentricity, the genesis of the African-centered educational movement preceded him. During the 1960s, the Black Nationalist and Black Power movements fostered a climate for agency and efficacy among African American communities. Consequently, African American parents began to seek control over the public education of their children that currently manifests in the demand for educational initiatives specific to the needs of African American children. The increasing interest in implementing an African-centered curriculum into the public schools has facilitated emergent definitions of what characterizes an African-centered curriculum. Theorist Asante's (1991) criterion for an African-centered curriculum mandates that it must "center" the students within their own cultural information.

Another theorist, Wade Nobles, a professor of Black Studies at San Francisco State University and one who designed and implemented an African-centered curriculum in a high school in Oakland, California, defined the objectives of an African-centered curriculum:

> A curriculum infused with African and African American content must systematically guide the transmission of information and knowledge while simultaneously reinforcing in African-American students the desire to learn and encouraging the adoption of behaviors and attitudes consistent with the historical excellence of African people. (Nobles, 1990, p. 10)

He further stated that an African-centered curriculum should fulfill several criteria:

> 1. Refer to the life experiences, history and traditions of African people as the center of analyses;

> 2. Utilize African and African American experience as the core paradigm for human liberation and higher-level human functioning; and

> 3. Assist African American students in the self-conscious act of creating history. (Nobles, 1990, p. 20)

Geoffrey Giddings (2001), a professor of African and African American Studies, studying the immersion of an African-centered curriculum into a traditional public school, summarized various researchers' perspectives on the criteria for an African-centered curriculum into five elements:

> 1. Assist students in developing the necessary intellectual, moral and emotional skills for accomplishing a productive, affirming life in this society.

> 2. Provide such educational instruction as to deconstruct established hegemonic pillars and to safeguard against the construction of new ones.

3. Provide students of African descent with educational instruction that uses techniques that are in accord with their learning styles.

4. Assist students of African descent in maintaining a positive self-concept, with the goal of achieving a sense of collective accountability.

5. Serve as a model for Banks' (1998) "Transformation" and "Social Action" approaches to multicultural education. (p. 463)

Kwame Agyei Akoto is the cofounder of a K–12 African-centered independent Black institution located in Washington, DC. With over 30 years of experience with an African-centered school, Akoto insists that an African-centered curriculum must be established on the tenets of nation building and liberation for African people. Akoto (1992) provided a concise definition of an African-centered curriculum in his work, *Nationbuilding: Theory and Practice in Afrikan Centered Education*. Akoto, in fact, developed the African Centered Thematic Inventory (ACTI) as a guideline to the "curricula domains" (p. 129) of an African-centered curriculum. He delineated five curricula domains for an African-centered education: (1) Cultural/ideological, (2) spiritual/psycho-affective, (3) sociopolitical and economic, (4) technological, and (5) nation building. Akoto contended that the purpose of an African-centered curriculum must be "(a) to advance the African American nationality, its cultural and ideological goals; and (b) to facilitate fully functional and/or exceptional performance in a white dominated American political economy" (p. 169).

As varied as the definitions of an African-centered curriculum appear to be, I discovered that many researchers and educators posit that this curriculum cannot effectively impact the lives of African American students unless it is instructed from African-centered pedagogy.

What Is African-Centered Pedagogy?

The term *pedagogy* is used in reference to the methodology employed in the instructions of curricula. Fundamental to the pedagogy utilized within the educational process are the values, perceptions, and philosophy of education. In the traditional schools, the pedagogy is shaped by the values of the dominant culture, a culture in which "normative" and "universal" are White and middle class. This pedagogical perspective is Eurocentric. It negates the cultural attributes of African American children and attempts to assimilate or acculturate the student into the dominant paradigm.

An African-centered curriculum provides the framework or guidelines for an African-centered education; however, the delivery of the instructions will impact the quality of an African-centered education. This instructional delivery is encompassed in the pedagogy utilized by the educational institution and is the pedagogy that teachers employ in their interactions with students. Various scholars and researchers have delineated the objectives of African-centered pedagogy (Akoto, 1994; Lee, 1994; Murrell, 2002).

In defining African-centered pedagogy, Peter Murrell (2002) explained that African American historical experience and cultural position must be a vital part of this pedagogy:

> [This pedagogy should] provide teachers with a unifying framework for how they are to apply understanding of human cognition, learning, and development…but also guide teachers in how to situate those understandings in practice—and to use these situated understanding[s] to take full account of the lives, histories, cultures, and worldviews of children in diverse urban communities. (p. x)

Murrell's perspective of African-centered pedagogy is one in which he does not focus so much on the teacher exhibiting the qualities of an African-centered pedagogy as he does on the "system of practices" that produces achievement outcomes for African American children (p. 16).

Carol Lee (1994) posited that African-centered pedagogy is critical to the education of African American children. She noted that this pedagogy is a necessary defense to the pervasive Eurocentric influences in education and society. She also iterated that African-centered pedagogy is needed "to produce an education that contributes to pride, equity, power, wealth, and cultural continuity for Africans in America and elsewhere" (p. 296). She put forth principles for an effective African-centered pedagogy:

1. Legitimizes African stores of knowledge;

2. Positively exploits and scaffolds productive community and cultural practices;

3. Extends and builds upon the indigenous language;

4. Reinforces community ties and idealizes service to one's family, community, nation, race, and world;

5. Promotes positive social relationships;

6. Imparts a world view that idealizes a positive, self-sufficient future for one's people without denying the self-worth and right to self-determination of others; and

7. Supports cultural continuity while promoting critical consciousness. (p. 297)

Lee also noted that African-centered pedagogy is established upon the principles of Maat, which is an Egyptian concept put forth by Maulana Karenga (1989). The principles of Maat acknowledge (a) the divine image of humans, (b) the perfectibility of humans, (c) the teachability of humans, (d) the free will of humans, and (e) the essentiality of moral social practice in human development (Lee, 1994, p. 297). Lee further stated that the cultivation of this paradigm is essential to the "resistance to political and cultural oppression but also to sustain independent development" (p. 297).

According to Akoto (1994), African-centered pedagogy "is concerned with the acquisition of self-determination and self-sufficiency for African people....It is ultimately concerned with truth and the 'African centered mission to humanize the universe'" (p. 321). African-centered pedagogy is not about adopting "ancient rituals, values, behaviors, and relationships that have no relevance to modernity" (Akoto, 1994, p. 323) but should highlight those traditions and values of former societies that benefit humanity irrespective of time and place:

> An African-centered pedagogy is a pedagogy derived from the African historical continuum and cultural dynamics. It endeavors to stimulate and nourish creative and critical consciousness and to inculcate through study and application a firm conscious commitment to the reconstruction of true African nation-hood, and the restoration of the African historical/cultural continuum. (Akoto, 1994, p. 325)

When considering African-centered pedagogy, several scholars have noted that the valuing system of Nguzo Saba is its foundation (Akoto, 1994; Kenyatta, 1998; Lee, 1994). This valuing system, also known as the Black Value System, was created by Karenga (1989) and comprises seven principles: (1) Umoja—unity, (2) kujichagulia—self-determination, (3) ujima—collective work and responsibility, (4) ujamaa—cooperative economics, (5) kuumba—creativity, (6) Nia—purpose, and (7) imani—faith (in one's self, one's family, and one's people). The utilization of these principles in African-centered pedagogy denotes that instructors must "commit to engage in democratic decision-making processes, have faith in the possibilities of leadership that each person possesses, and dedicate themselves to serving the African American community" (Lee, 1992, p. 167).

Akoto (1994) and Lee (1992) asserted that a critical element in African-centered pedagogy is the teacher, who is the transmitter of culture. This point is further illuminated by Lee, who noted that having a knowledge of Black history and a love for children does not guarantee that a teacher can "effectively teach using an Afrocentric pedagogy" (p. 167). Shujaa (1994) substantiated this point that teachers are crucial to an African-centered education through the utilization of African-centered pedagogy. He asserted the following:

> Working with and in independent African centered schools for nearly 20 years I have seen good teachers grounded in African-centered thinking use European-centered racist materials to teach brilliant African-centered lessons. I have seen European-American as well as some African-American public school teachers grounded in European-centered thinking use curriculum materials written by our best African-centered thinkers in ways that trivialize and mis-represent the content. These experiences have convinced me that it is the African-centeredness of the teacher's thinking that determines the African-centeredness of the teaching. (p. 256)

As clearly expressed by the aforementioned researchers, African-centered pedagogy must recognize the cultural specificity of the African American community and its continuation. This pedagogy has to facilitate the holistic development of the student by the recognition and valuation of the student's language, culture, and cognitive styles, as well as cultivate his or her ability to create history. Now, how does African-centered pedagogy and an African-centered curriculum contribute to an African-centered educational model?

African-Centered Educational Model

Traditional education in America has been instituted with the objective of inculcating the values, norms, and beliefs of the dominant culture, for example, European Americans. "Formal educational systems," according to Akoto (1992), "are integral organs of the nation-state and of the cultural ethos that engenders that state" (p. 45). As a nation-state, America's educational system operates as a vehicle of perpetuation for the cultural, sociopolitical, and economical structures of the dominant ideology (Ballantine & Hammack, 2011; Carnoy, 1974). Traditional public schools provide instructions to students from a White nationalist curriculum while utilizing a Eurocentric pedagogy for its delivery. This pedagogy uses methodology that delivers instruction from a Eurocentric perspective, utilizing the values and norms attributed to European Americans or the dominant ideology in a hegemonic methodology. The cultural and historical epistemologies of the students of color are not considered in giving instructions and the knowledge is delivered from a Eurocentric bias.

The consensus by many scholars, educators, and parents in the African American community is that an African-centered curriculum should be immersed within the traditional school curriculum. An African-centered curriculum can provide the guidelines for instructions for students of various ages and ethnicities, specifically for African American students who now comprise the majority population in urban schools in most major metropolitan areas. However, the immersion of an African-centered curriculum without the complement of African-centered pedagogy will not provide African American children with an African-centered education.

In many schools where an African-centered curriculum has been infused in instruction, it has been ineffectual in improving academic outcomes. In most cases, the missing component is African-centered pedagogy. When African-centered pedagogy is neglected in teaching an African-centered curriculum, the result is not an African-centered education but an education that is Eurocentric in presentation and results. Teaching history using African-centered facts but presenting those facts from a Eurocentric worldview will situate the African American child on the periphery of Europe as an object rather than a subject of history (Asante, 1991).

Many researchers challenge the authenticity of the African-centered educational models that are currently implemented in charter schools and traditional public schools (Akoto, 1994; Lee, 1992; Lomotey, 1992). These researchers argue that these curriculum models do not address a key component of an African-centered education, which is "maintaining and perpetuating the African culture throughout the nation building process" (Hotep, 2001, p. 212). This effort to promote the African cultural continuum must be manifested through nation building, the transmission of values, and the acknowledgment of African spirituality. In fact, these researchers contend that an authentic African-centered educational model cannot be taught within the mainstream school system (Akoto, 1994; Hotep, 2001; Lee, 1992; Lomotey, 1992).

This educational model requires teachers who are consciously engaged in the African-centered personal transformation, who acknowledge and cultivate the spirituality of African people, and who can deliver the instructions with African-centered pedagogy (Akoto, 1994; Hotep, 2001; Shujaa, 1994). At present, there are no teacher preparation programs in traditional college settings that are preparing teachers to teach an African-centered educational model. It is the contention of these researchers and also leaders in the Council of Independent Black Institutions (CIBI) that the African-centered educational model that emerged with the advent of Independent Black Institutions (IBIs) has been adulterated and co-opted into the public school setting (Akoto, 1994; Hotep, 2001; Lee, 1992; Lomotey, 1992). Metaphorically, it is like taking a branch from an oak tree and then presenting the branch to the world as the oak tree.

Drawing on the aforementioned research, I found that an African-centered educational model must consist of both the African-centered curriculum and the African-centered pedagogy, which will enable the promotion and nurturance of the concept of Afrocentricity, or a centering of African descendants as subjects of their history. The results of this research have convinced me of the necessity of the deliberate formation of this model. Now that my understanding has been enlightened through the literature of what an authentic African-centered educational model should be, I decided to continue in the discovery of how this model has been implemented in contemporary times. The next section provides details of how this model has been implemented in various methods in recent times.

Building a Shelf to Sell the Crystals

"When you want something, all the universe conspires in helping you to achieve it," he had said. (Coelho & Clarke, 1988/1993, p. 29)

Now that I had more clearly defined the concept of the African-centered educational model, I thought that I would explore the implementation of this model. Once again, I dove into the literature to discover the ways that African Americans had attempted to implement this model into their educational experiences and the experiences of their children. I quickly found that this model had been implemented in various venues, such as IBIs, charter schools, and traditional public schools. In the following section, I provide an overview of African American efforts to implement this educational model into contemporary education.

Contemporary Options in African-Centered Education

With the passing of the *Brown v. Board of Education* legislation, African Americans wanted to believe that America's espoused values of democratic morality had triumphed over racism. This idealism sought to rationalize America's past abuses with the hope that its national conscience would acknowledge the humanity of African Americans by providing them with a quality education and bestowing them with first-class citizenship status.

However, African Americans soon discovered that the privilege of sharing a classroom with European Americans was not to be without concessions on their part. African Americans had to relinquish their own schools and their own teachers.

The integration and desegregation of schools did not achieve the educational outcomes that many African Americans had hoped for, and by the early 1970s, African Americans found their schools as segregated as they had been before the *Brown* decision. The condition of the schools had only minimally improved. Many of the schools in the African American communities were closed, and African American students were bused to European American schools. Consequently, the academic achievement for African American students did not increase substantially as had been hoped for by the proponents of the *Brown* decision. Once again, African American parents began to look for alternatives in educating their children, particularly in African-centered schools.

The realization that American public schools had made little progress in providing an equitable education for African American students reignited grassroots efforts within many African American communities to ensure the education of their children. Historically, these efforts had never ceased; however, the betrayal of the African American community by the legal, social, and educational structures intensified the struggle for equitable and meaningful education for African American children. After the *Brown* decision, the first schools that offered an African-centered educational model for African American students were IBIs.

Independent Black Institutions

While the Black Power movement was spreading throughout African American communities within America during the 1960s, African American parents began to seek control over the public education for their children. A significant example of this push for community control took place in New York City with the Ocean Hill-Brownsville controversy (Doughty, 1973; Hotep, 2001; Lomotey, 1992), where African American parents and other community leaders sought to establish local control of the public schools in their community. This effort was met with conflict and resistance and resulted in community leaders starting Uhuru Sasa, one of the first IBIs (Hotep, 2001; Lomotey, 1992; Ratteray & Shujaa, 1987).

The success of Uhuru Sasa precipitated the establishment of many IBIs within New York and throughout the United States (Hotep, 2001). These schools were started as small, private schools, afterschool programs, and Saturday schools. Oftentimes, IBIs were started by parents who were frustrated with the lack of local control over public schools and the curriculum (Lee, 1992; Lomotey, 1992). For the most part, these schools were supported by the communities in which they were established through donations or through low cost tuition. They have small enrollments, generally 50 to 200 students (Lomotey, 1992).

The curricula in these schools were often African centered because parents and educators were looking for innovative and culturally relevant ways to ameliorate the education of African American children (Lee, 1992; Lomotey, 1992). In an effort to establish a standard African-centered educational model and provide resources and ideas to other IBIs, a unifying organization was formed. In June of 1972, the CIBI was created in Frogmore, South Carolina (Doughty, 1973). According to Hotep (2001), the mission of the CIBI has these requirements:

> [B]uilding Pan African nationalist educational institutions rooted in not only academic excellence, but also self-reliance and self-definition, not for mainstream integration, but for independent nation building, that sets it apart from all other educational institutions that serve the African American community (p. 35). The educational philosophy of the IBIs reflects the integration of the ideologies of Black Nationalism (self-determination), Pan Africanism (unity), and Black Power (agency) in the emphasis of three areas for an optimal student educational experience:
>
> 1. Creating a strong family and community cohesion,
>
> 2. Incorporating the value system of Maat and Nguzo Saba (Kiswahili for "The Seven Principles of Blackness") introduced by Maulana Karenga (1988), and
>
> 3. By what Lomotey (1992) refers to as "Revolutionary Pan-African Nationalism." (p. 458)

The creation of strong family and community cohesion is encouraged through the tradition of students referring to teachers in Kiswahili familial terms of baba (father) and mama (mother). Teachers are encouraged and expected to treat their students as if they were their own children (Lee, 1992; Lomotey, 1992). Also, parents are expected to be involved with the community of the school. In fact, the IBIs understood that accepting a child into the school was in effect adopting that child as part of the school family, with all of the rights and obligations. So parents were found working in the office, on committees, and in the classrooms.

The IBIs use the value system of Kawaida, a system of formal teachings de-rived from ancient African philosophy that was introduced into the African American community by Karenga (1989). Doughty (1973) asserted that Kawaida is both "a religion as well as an ideology" (p. 98). He further expli-cated that Kawaida provides a value system that assists African Americans in self-determination, self-respect, and self-identity. The Nguzo Saba principles are values associated with the Kawaida faith. According to Doughty (1973), "as a part of Kawaida, the Nguzo Saba is a describer of life, how one lives, in what manner and for what reasons" (p. 99).

Maat is also a value system of the Kawaida philosophy, incorporated within the IBIs' educational philosophy. Maat is a formal system of character instructions that is expressed in the "Seven Cardinal Virtues of truth, justice, propriety, harmony, balance, reciprocity and order" (Karenga, 1989, p. 37). The IBIs utilize various activities to inculcate these values into the daily learning experiences of their students, parents, and staff.

Revolutionary Pan-African Nationalism is "part of a new system of ed-ucation to replace the existing 'mainstream' system that is inappropriate for African Americans, provide[s] a means by which African Americans can identify with Africans around the world, and acknowledge[s] the view that African Americans make up a nation within a nation" (Lomotey, 1992, p. 458). This ideology is fundamental to the objectives of nation building, self-determination, and the unification of Africans throughout the diaspora and is emphasized throughout the educational experience.

IBIs can be found throughout the nation. However, because these schools are tuition based, only a small percentage of African American parents can afford to send their children to them. Recently, the charter school movement has provided another option for the African American community to provide equitable and appropriate education for their children.

African-Centered Charter Schools

The charter school movement started in the early 1990s as a school reform effort. Policymakers and parents were concerned that bureaucracy and large student populations hindered schools from being productive and efficient. Charter schools are independent public school academies that receive their charters from chartering agencies and are managed by groups and organi-zations rather than the central office of a traditional school district. These schools are initiated by teachers, parents, educators, community leaders, for-profit companies, and other community stakeholders (Murrell, 1999). These schools hire their own teachers and develop their own curriculum; however, their students are not exempt from meeting the state's educational standards in which proficiency is demonstrated through standardized testing.

African-centered charter schools, which have been established across the nation, were created by parents, community leaders, and educators who wanted to exercise control over the education of their children. These stakeholders were not only interested in exercising agency; they also wanted their children to learn about their African heritage. Generally, these charter schools have a small student enrollment similar to the independent Black schools and are concentrated in the K–8 grade levels. Unlike the independent Black schools, charter schools receive per-student public funding from the same sources as public schools.

The exercise of autonomy over the structure of African-centered charter schools has not proceeded without a challenge (Watson & Smitherman, 1996). In one instance, Detroit, Michigan, attempted to start an all-male charter school that would specifically target educating the African American male population. Research had revealed that this particular student population was experiencing an alarming rate of school difficulties, but state law prohibited the Detroit school district from operating this all-male school and forced the proposed schools to open enrollment to all students (Watson & Smitherman, 1996).

These African-centered charter schools have experienced some academic success with African American students (Rockquemore, 1997). However, the No Child Left Behind legislation has caused tension by creating a dichotomy of goals for the schools. The charter school community must determine how to continue to maintain an African-centered educational focus, while teaching to the state standardized test. Substantiating this difficulty, Murrell (1999) found that African-centered charter schools often succumb to the pressure of ensuring that students achieve on the state's standardized test and lessen their African-centered focus. The end result is "school as usual," in other words, an educational experience for the student that is no different from a traditional public school education.

The charter school movement provided alternative educational opportunities for African American children; yet similar to IBIs, they were limited in their ability to reach the large populations of African American children in urban schools in large metropolitan areas. Grassroots efforts in the mid-1990s provided the momentum to implement African-centered educational models within traditional public schools, where African American students were the predominant student population, most often in large urban centers.

African-Centered Traditional Public Schools

Around the mid-1990s, there was a concerted effort to implement African-centered education within traditional public schools in urban centers such as Milwaukee, Portland, Philadelphia, Newark, Detroit, Oakland, and Washington, DC. (Ginwright, 1999; Murrell, 1999; Pollard & Ajirotutu, 2000). This model of implementation was referred to as African-centered immersion projects. The impetus for this movement within urban schools was rooted in the frustrations of African American parents and community leaders with the continued failings of African American students, particularly African American males. White flight from and de-industrialization in urban centers created urban school environments in which these schools were underfunded, and the student population became predominantly composed of children of color. In fact, studies have demonstrated that children of color, specifically African American children, are now more likely to attend predominantly African American schools than before the *Brown* decision (Darling-Hammond, 2014; Orfield, Eaton, & Harvard Project on School Desegregation, 1996).

For parents residing in these urban settings, options to acquire an equitable education for their children through access to private schools or African-centered charter schools did not exist because of their inability to afford tuition or provide transportation to these schools. Coupled with the urgency of ameliorating the crisis of African American males as manifested in high dropout rates, high suspension rates, and underachievement, African American parents, educators, and community activists confronted school boards and demanded the immersion of an African-centered curriculum into traditional public schools. The rationale for this demand was that students receiving instruction from a culturally relevant curriculum would enhance learning by providing an environment in which students were not alienated from the instruction and materials presented (Asante, 1991).

In summary, the African-centered educational movement has been in the hearts of African Americans from the beginning of civilization in Africa. Although not given the term African centered to describe it, it was African centered simply because Africans were the subjects of their own history.

Since the initial contact with Europeans and involuntary sojourn to America, Africans have fought to maintain their humanity through education. As if they understood that the universe was working to give them the thing that they desired, Africans sought to cocreate with their Creator to

bring their desires into manifestation. Whether through education by organized efforts of free Blacks or through stolen moments in the night, African
Americans have been determined to acquire the key that would open the
door to liberty. When the key did not give them access to that liberty because
the enactment of federal and state legislature created barriers to first-class citizenship, they contemplated education for a separate nation, whether in the
United States or in the motherland.

The *Brown* decision renewed hope for African Americans in the belief
that America could be a "united" nation. By the 1980s, however, African
Americans knew that once again they had experienced "a dream deferred."
Consequently, grassroots organizations in many African American communities comprising teachers, parents, and community members began pushing
for African-centered education for their children, whether in IBIs, African-
centered charter schools, or African-centered immersion projects in traditional public schools.

4. LOCATING THE CARAVAN TO EGYPT

"It's called the principle of favorability, beginner's luck. Because life wants you to achieve your destiny," the old king had said. (Coelho & Clarke, 1988/1933, p. 35)

This extensive review of the literature gave me significant insight into and respect toward the intrinsic human desire of African Americans for self-determination. I feel that the "principle of favorability" has gifted me with fundamental information that peeled back the layers around this educational model. Like Santiago, I was feeling that luck was on my side and was assisting me in answering the question that I had posed at the onset of this search. I felt that I wanted to understand the perceived value of this educational model on the lives of African American students. I wanted to address the following questions: Is there more for students to gain from this educational model than just higher grades? Does this educational model enhance self-concept and increase life's opportunities for students who attend an African-centered school for a majority of their educational career?

However, I believed the question I really needed to ask was this: "How do African American students who have graduated from an African-centered school perceive that school experience in retrospect?" I take a moment to reflect on *The Alchemist* once again. As Santiago steps out to fulfill his dream, he encounters an old man whose name is Melchizedek. Melchizedek informs Santiago of the principle of favorability, which he explains as the belief that life is working to help you fulfill your destiny. This became important to me as I was faced with the need to locate a school and participants who would fit the criteria for my research. Yes!

Now that I could clearly understand that others had attempted to answer this question long before I had thought to ask it, I knew I was moving to the next step of this journey, which was to locate a school that was established in this educational model and provide students with this experience. So I began to search for schools that were teaching students using this African-centered educational model. I quickly became aware that there were a small number of these schools in the United States serving small numbers of African American children at the time of my research, and the numbers were rapidly dwindling. As I previously mentioned, many of these schools were IBIs or charter schools (Lomotey, 1992; Murrell, 1999). There were a small number of traditional public schools that had immersed African-centered curricula into the traditional curriculum (Pollard & Ajirotutu, 2000).

The universe was conspiring to assist me in getting what I wanted. Little did I know that I would encounter an informant at the university who would be the key to locating the ideal school that I was seeking and even had the participants who would meet the research criteria.

When I considered a site for my study, I had several constraints that were overshadowing the decision for its location. I lived in a city that had no schools teaching students from an African-centered educational model; however, 60 miles away was a city that had six African-centered schools in operation. Although I was aware of African-centered home schools in that area, I was not able to confirm those numbers at the time of this study. Three of the schools had been IBIs and had converted to charter schools during the early to mid-1990s. The other three schools were created as African-centered public schools.

The setting for this research was in a K–12 charter school situated within an urban community about 60 miles from my residence in the Midwest. The Faizah Shule/Marcus Garvey Preparatory Academy[1] (FS/MGPA) was an African-centered charter school that provided instruction to students from kindergarten through 12th grade. The high school was named the Marcus Garvey Preparatory Academy (MGPA) and emphasized student preparation for higher education from an African-centered educational model. It was located in a large, metropolitan city in Michigan.

I knew that I would need someone to mediate my introduction to the school director and assist me in locating former students from the school. These concerns required me to actively locate a site with a reasonable commuting distance, and I wasn't really thinking about traveling more than an hour one way to get to any destination. I suppose I was just being lazy about the travel, but I couldn't seem to convince myself to acquiesce to more than an hour on the road one way. So after a brief inquiry in the African and African American Studies program at Michigan State University, I hit the jackpot and was connected to a fellow doctoral student in that department who became my informant for this study. He was instrumental in introducing me to several potential participants as well as assisting me in gaining access to the school.

The FS/MGPA was selected because it had been established and was operating for well over 40 years, first as an independent school and later as a charter school. Other factors that made this site palatable include the following: (a) I was happy with the fact that it was no more than an hour drive from my home; (b) I had an informant who was well acquainted with the school environment; and (c) there was a pool of former students who could be participants in my study. My informant had been employed in various capacities in the school for well over 20 years.

The fact that this school had been operating for a substantial period of time was very significant. Research revealed that curriculum, whether new or well-established, can have a direct impact on educational outcomes for students in an African-centered program (Ginwright, 1999; Pollard & Ajirutoto, 2000). Also, this school offered an educational experience for students from kindergarten through 12th grade. This would ensure the likelihood of finding young people for the study who had spent the majority of their educational career in the African-centered school, which was critical to understanding the impact of the experience.

Participants

Historically, MGPA maintained a small graduating class, beginning with its first graduation of seven students in 1996. Each year thereafter, the graduating class ranged from 7 to 15 students, resulting in the graduation of approximately 120 students by June 2005. At the time that I engaged in the study, the high school had an enrollment of approximately 60 students, 9 of them seniors. I was able to locate and interview seven former students regarding their educational experience at this African-centered school.

As mentioned earlier, a former teacher facilitated my efforts to locate students who had this educational experience and for the study (Glesne, 1999). Initially, with this teacher's assistance, I was able to contact three former students. However upon utilizing criterion and snowball sampling (Miles & Huberman, 1994), I was able to locate six more former students, for a total of nine. Seven of the total students located agreed to participate in the study. Locating participants for the study was somewhat problematic because most of the students who had graduated from the high school were either away at college, had moved to another state, or were difficult to locate. The seven participants consisted of two brothers from the same family, a brother and sister from another family, and three individual participants. The participants were from middle-class and working-class families, and at least one parent of each participant had graduated from college. Three of the participants graduated from high school in 1996, three graduated in 2001, and one graduated in 2002.

The seven former students were located and interviewed in an effort to understand their perceptions of their educational experience at an African-centered school. I was able to engage each participant in 60- to 90-minute intensive in-depth interviews. From the data collected, I was able to garner common themes and patterns, which emerged as significant components of the educational experience of these young people. From the findings, I decided that narratives were the optimal way to relay their stories. Ochs and Capps (1996) confirmed that narrative "provides tellers with an opportunity to impose order on otherwise disconnected events, and to create continuity between past, present, and imagined worlds" (p. 22).

In the next chapter, I use the narratives to share the perspectives of the various players in shaping the story of this educational experience. First, I provide a brief overview of the school. Next, I invite you to meet the founder of the school and experience her passion and commitment toward bringing her dream to fruition. I was intrigued with the founder's story because she modeled the grit and determination that fulfilling a passion is most likely to demand of a person. As Santiago reflected on the attainment of his dreams, he regarded the struggles along the road:

Tell your heart that the fear of suffering is worse than the suffering itself. And that no heart has ever suffered when it goes in search of its dreams, because every second of the search is a second's encounter with God and with eternity. (Coelho & Clarke, 1988/1993, p. 89)

However, I do not stop there. I transport you into a day in the life of the school. Yes, you become a *mwanafunzi* (student) and mentally join with the students in their daily experiences.

5. LOCATING THE TREASURE

Everything on earth is being continuously transformed, because the earth is alive...and it has a soul. We are part of that soul, so we rarely recognize that it is working for us. (Coelho & Clarke, 1988/1993, p. 53)

The Freedom City School District (FCSD), where the FS/MGPA is located, has a student enrollment of approximately 170,000; well over 90% of its student population is African American. By the 2001–2002 academic year, more than 19,000 students were attending charter schools in Freedom City. In an effort to minimize the impact of declining enrollment resulting from students transferring to charter schools, the FCSD capped the FS/MGPA's student enrollment at 300. During the 2004–2005 academic year, the school had a student enrollment of 260 (Aisha Shule/W. E. B. Du Bois Preparatory Academy, 2005).

FS/MGPA began in 1974 as an IBI in the format of a Saturday School. It was named the Nat Turner School; its genesis was rooted in the Black Power, Black Nationalist, and Pan-Africanist movements of the 1960s, as African Americans were redefining themselves and their existence in American society. These movements were both political and economic within African American communities, and they promoted the ideology that Black people on the continent and the diaspora must become self-determined and self-reliant.

In response to this movement, a collective of parents, educators, and professionals began to embrace the self-determination initiative to create the private school.

When the Nat Turner School became a full day school in 1976, the name was changed to the Faizah Shule Academy for Gifted Children. The name of the school was significant for two reasons. First, the name was changed to *Faizah Shule* because "Faizah" is a Kiswahili term for *life*, and *Shule* is Kiswahili for *school*. In essence, the name "Faizah Shule" means the "school of life." The second reason the name was changed was to give emphasis to the African-centered educational model and to stress the philosophy of the school, which emanated from the philosophy of Mama Taraji, the founder and director of the school. Mama Taraji held the belief that African American children were gifted and that their school experience should be holistic and should impact every aspect of each child's life. In that same year, the Faizah Shule joined the CIBI and was instrumental in refining the ideology of IBIs that consequently resulted in facilitating the creation of national standards for them.

As an IBI, student enrollment for Faizah Shule comprised approximately 60 students. The requirement for attending the Faizah Shule was through parental choice and student tuition. Whenever possible, scholarships were awarded to families who experienced temporary financial hardships. Rather than have the students leave the African-centered learning environment to attend public school, when the oldest students reached the 8th grade, the Shule extended its grades each year until the school reached the 12th grade. When the high school was added, it was named the Marcus Garvey Preparatory Academy and emphasized student preparation for higher education. Although the schools were located in separate buildings, they were usually presented as one entity, the FS/MGPA, when Mama Taraji referenced them. In 1996, the FS/MGPA experienced its first graduating class of seven students.

The Faizah Shule—Background

The Faizah Shule was located in the building that housed K–8 grades and had been a storefront that encompassed the entire length of a short city block. Christian churches of various denominations lined the streets like trees on both sides of the Shule and across the street from it. The building was painted dark red and windows lined the front, the left side, and the back of it. Each window was shielded from unwanted entry by cast iron security rails. A sign, "Faizah Shule/Marcus Garvey Preparatory Academy," hung over the main entrance of the school.

The school was divided into two learning circles. One was the Nile Valley Learning Circle, where students were instructed from kindergarten through fifth grade. This learning circle was located at one end of the building and consisted of open classrooms that were divided by material cabinets, lockers, and coat racks for the younger students. The room was painted white. The classroom walls were utilized for student achievements, decorated bulletin boards, affirmation posters, African American historical figures, and various maps of the world, particularly the continent of Africa. Within the Nile Valley Learning Circle, grades were identified by West African ethnic (tribal) groups.

The second learning circle was the Pyramid Learning Circle, where students were instructed from sixth through eighth grade. This learning group was located at the opposite end of the building. Along the narrow hall that connected both instructional centers were offices for the finance managers, the school psychologist, counselors, and instructors. The office for the director and the administrative assistant was located in the same area as the Pyramid Learning Circle. There were three rooms in this area that were utilized for instruction: one main room and two adjacent rooms—one on each side of the main room. Off from the main room was an area with about eight computers. During the times that I visited the Shule, I never observed any students using the computers. Mama Taraji is a constant presence passing through the rooms, occasionally stopping to praise, or if necessary, chastise students.

Marcus Garvey Preparatory Academy—Background

The Marcus Garvey Preparatory Academy was housed in a building located on the property of the oldest African American college in Freedom City. Leased in 1994, it was located to the left of the main building on the property. The building had multiple levels, with rooms on all floors. The front exterior wall of the building was brick and the side walls and back wall were covered with painted white wood. Windows flanked the front of the building, with a few located on the sides and in the rear. The front entrance was always locked and could be accessed only from the parking lot that also served the college. The rear of the building had a gated perimeter.

Displayed on a small table in the foyer was a picture of the school's name-sake, Marcus Garvey. Also displayed on the table was the official accreditation of the Marcus Garvey Academy as a member of the National Honors Society, along with African statues and artifacts. In this building, there were three classrooms on the upper level of the school and three on the bottom level. At one time, this building served as the elementary school; later it would become the high school.

> What you still need to know is this: before a dream is realized, the Soul of the World tests everything that was learned along the way. It does this not because it is evil, but so that we can, in addition to realizing our dreams, master the lessons we've learned as we've moved toward that dream. That's the point at which most people give up. It's the point at which, as we say in the language of the desert, one "dies of thirst just when the palm trees have appeared on the horizon." (Coelho & Clarke, 1988/1993, p. 91–92)

Meeting the Queen of the Shule

To understand the context of the FS/MGPA, it is necessary to first meet and interact with the founder of the school. The vision of the school is enmeshed and embedded intricately within her social, historical, political, and cultural perspective. So our effort to explore the context of the school must occur simultaneously with understanding the founder, Mama Taraji.

I remember that I was astonished at the physical beauty and stamina of Mama Taraji, a beautiful woman in her 70s when we met. She was medium stature and, upon our first meeting, was attired in a colorful African top and slacks. Her long gray locks flowed from under her headdress. She was soft-spoken with a calm and warm demeanor. A native of Freedom City, she grew up during a time when the African American community of the city was rich and vibrant with the presence of African American cultural heritage:

> And we went to everything…all cultural groups [because] at that time people came to churches in community things and anybody could go. There were Black business and science expositions…that [were] kind of in with George Washington Carver people. Black inventions and Black businesses, people got to see those…. And in the Black community there was a race consciousness that was different than it is now, I think. We knew about Marcus Garvey, W. E. B. Du Bois…. We got to see Eartha Kitt… Lena Horne…I mean we just had these images of Black people who were prominent and successful in all areas…from athletes to inventors to intellectuals. (personal communication, 2004)

After graduating from high school, she continued on to college where she co-majored in English and French. She taught English and journalism in the FCSD for 10 years. She decided to pursue a master's degree and began substitute teaching throughout the Freedom City School District. During this time, she witnessed the economic and subsequent resource disparity between affluent and low socioeconomic schools and decided that she needed to create her own school. She noted that her drive for the advocacy of African American children stimulated her search for an educational model that would address their specific concerns. She asserted the following: "I was looking for something that would dramatically impact [African American] students." (personal communication, 2004)

In 1974, Mama Taraji, along with a collective of 12 families, opened the school that would eventually become Faizah Shule as a Saturday School called the Nat Turner School. Mama Taraji described the process of the genesis and evolution of the Saturday school:

> The process that we chose was to run a Saturday school for two years and to develop and test curriculum…at least one member of the family was an educator. And most of them taught higher education, they were college instructors and professors. So we worked diligently and seriously on curriculum and we tested it in six week segments. We had kids come for six weeks and then they were off for a week while [we] did an evaluation and assessment, rewrote or wrote core curriculum until we had felt strong enough and we were ready to open the Shule in 1974. (personal communication, 2005)

In 1976, yielding to increased pressure from parents and having refined the curriculum, the Saturday School became a full K–8 school and the name was changed to Faizah Shule.

Struggles: The Tool of Perfection

Historically, Mama Taraji and the Shule community struggled to keep the school open, and this struggle was manifested in constant relocation of the school. In over 30 years of existence, the school moved nine times. The Shule began in an Episcopal Church center and after several years moved to a Lutheran Church. After a brief period, the Shule moved to Lorne College of Business. Violations cited by the fire marshal caused the Shule to move again. A small building was purchased but then lost due to financial difficulties. Next, the Shule moved to a Catholic Church. The church decided to demolish the building and the Shule was forced to move again, this time to another Lutheran Church. Officials at the Lutheran Church decided to terminate the lease and the Shule moved to the Young Women's Christian Association (YWCA). The YWCA eventually closed and the Shule moved to the Young Men's Christian Association (YMCA). After several years, the YMCA closed and was sold to Catholic housing. Finally, the Shule moved back to Lorne College of Business, which is its current location.

In 1995, the Shule became a charter school and opened its enrollment to students within the FCSD.

The Guiding Principles for the Educational Experience

During this time, the school was under the ideological and organizational umbrella of the CIBI. In 1994, through the collaborative efforts of its members, in which Mama Taraji and the staff were instrumental, the CIBI created a position statement. The position statement defined an African-centered education, and in 1995, the CIBI also created national standards for evaluating African-centered educational institutions (Hotep, 2001). The definition, which follows, was created by CIBI, adopted by Faizah Shule, and guided the instructional pedagogy of its member schools:

> CIBI defines African-centered education as the means by which African culture—including the knowledge, attitudes, values and skills needed to maintain and perpetuate it throughout the nation building process—is developed and advanced through practice. Its aim, therefore, is to build commitment and competency within present and future generations to support the struggle for liberation and nationhood. We define nation building as the conscious and focused application of our people's collective resources, energies, and knowledge to the task of liberating and developing the psychic and physical space that we identify as ours. Nation building encompasses both the reconstruction of African culture and the development of a progressive and sovereign state structure consistent with that culture. (Hotep, 2001, p. 212)

The CIBI position statement further elucidates 10 beliefs for utilizing an African-centered education. The practice of African-centered education:

1. Acknowledges African spirituality as an essential aspect of our uniqueness as a people and makes it an instrument of our liberation;

2. Facilitates participation in the affairs of nations and defining (or redefining), reality on our own terms, in our own time and in our own interests;

3. Prepares Africans "for self-reliance, nation maintenance, and nation management in every regard";

4. Emphasizes the fundamental relationship between the strength of our families and the strength of our nation;

5. Ensures that the historic role and function of the customs, traditions, rituals and ceremonies—that have protected and preserved our culture; facilitated our spiritual expression; ensured harmony in our social relations; prepared our people to meet their responsibilities as adult members of our culture; and, sustained the continuity of African life over successive generations—are understood and made relevant to the challenges that confront us in our time;

6. Emphasizes that African identity is embedded in the continuity of African cultural history and that African cultural history represents a distinct reality continually evolving from the experiences of all African people wherever they are and have been on the planet across time and generations;

7. Focuses on the "knowledge and discovery of historical truths; through comparisons; hypothesizing and testing through debate, trial and application; through analysis and synthesis; through creative and critical thinking; through problem resolution processes; and through final evaluation and decision making";

8. Can only be systematically facilitated by people who themselves are consciously engaged in the process of African-centered personal transformation;

9. Is a process dependent upon human perception and interpretation (thus, it follows that a curriculum cannot be African-centered independent of our capacity to perceive and interpret it in an African-centered manner);

10. Embraces the traditional wisdom that "children are the reward of life" and it is, therefore, an expression of our unconditional love for them. In order to best serve African children our methods must reflect the best understanding we have of how they develop and learn biologically, spiritually and culturally. (Hotep, 2001, p. 212)

Integrating the beliefs and the position statement from the CIBI with her personal educational philosophy, Mama Taraji developed a framework for instructing students at the Faizah Shule. She articulated her educational philosophy as follows:

Our philosophy has evolved over the years. We have a collective philosophy. Basically, we are saying that we believe that all children are gifted. It is up to the teachers to identify and this is before Howard Gardner, to identify the particular strengths and talents in each child. And to develop a curriculum just for him alone that will become an equalizing factor for his social and academic growth, for these children. We believe in the whole child and that everything has to be addressed, the child's nutrition, the spiritual, the physical development, the intellect, etc. And because we live in a racist society, we believe that Black children need more intense mentoring...We believe that the parent should be involved at all levels from pre-school thru high school and probably on into college in their child's education...[because] their first teacher should continue to guide them, to study with them, to nurture them, to see that they have these things. (personal communication, 2004).

A more formal articulation of the educational philosophy of Faizah Shule/ Marcus Garvey Academy was located in the Parent Handbook (Aisha Shule/W. E. B. Du Bois Preparatory Academy, 1999) and reads as follows:

- We believe, as Dr. W. E. B. Du Bois believed, in preparing talented young people to provide leadership and service for African people at home and abroad. Our commitment is to continue this legacy within an African centered framework and a violence-free environment challenging students to become some of the finest scholars, artists, and leaders in the global community.
- We believe that with the spiritual and moral strength inherited from our ancestors, and through on-going struggle for justice, peace, and self-determination, the [Garvey] Preparatory experience will foster in the students a spirit of self-reliance and commitment to the rebuilding of our communities and reclaiming our traditional greatness.
- We believe that education is the gateway to liberation and that all students deserve to be fully and correctly educated with the truth of human endeavor. In the spirit of Sankofan Education, we must teach our students to reclaim and reconstruct African greatness, using that knowledge to establish working relationships with African people throughout the Diaspora.
- We believe that education is a transformative and life-long process. Growth through learning places responsibility on both Mwalimu (teacher) and Mwanafunzi (student) to share their knowledge and skills. This process involves social interaction, cultural immersion, hands-on, and "beyond the walls" creative school experiences that complement and reinforce reading, computing and research. Learning must be balanced between structure and freedom to create.
- We believe that parents must continue to take an active role throughout their children's entire education; and that parents and teachers must

work together to promote harmony, self-determination, cooperation, collective responsibility, purpose, creativity, and faith (the principles of the NGUZO SABA) in the children they collectively serve.

• We believe that all children deserve respect and protection; but must also learn to respect others. These lessons are best taught through role-modeling by adults who are positive and fair and consistent in their behavior.

• We believe that given an educational experience that promotes self-esteem, self-respect, and self-determination, and armed with a consciousness based on truth, justice, and service, African descended children can become competent and confident leaders in their communities and in a world of many diverse peoples and cultures. (p. 3)

The FS/MGPA has also developed a sevenfold purpose statement that reads as follows:

• To develop a learning model that encourages academic excellence, self-determination, entrepreneurship and social responsibility.

• To produce leadership for the re-development of the African American community.

• To reinforce group identity and pride as well as self-esteem by daily use of exemplary deeds and virtuous thoughts from great African people throughout our history.

• To instill a sense of belonging in parents, students, and teachers by emphasizing the concept of extended family.

• To develop strategic thinking based on past and present successes and creative possibilities for the future.

• To prepare students for higher learning.

• To examine the benefits of extended exposure of learners to education based on Afrocentric principles. (Aisha Shule/W. E. B. Du Bois Preparatory Academy, 1999, p. 4)

These documents were utilized as the guiding principles to ensure that students who attended the FS/MGPA received an African-centered educational experience. The overall intent of this experience was to produce leaders who were grounded in African culture and identity and who would work toward the liberation and perpetuation of African people on the continent and in the diaspora.

The next section provides detailed insight into the culture of a typical day in the Shule. The section provides a rich description of the rituals and ceremonies in which students were expected to engage as well as the songs and affirmations that students sang and recited each day in this educational experience.

A Typical Day in the Shule

Because people become fascinated with pictures and words, and wind up forgetting the Language of the World. (Coelho & Clarke, 1988/1993, p. 59)

Because the participants' memories of the Shule experience spanned a period of time, in some cases as many as 9 to 12 years, and also because the Shule has experienced various changes over the years, such as expanding grade levels and even converting to a charter school, the participants' descriptions of a typical day at the Shule have been synthesized. To provide a detailed representation of daily activities at the Shule, the synthesis of these memories is used to paint a portrait of a typical day.

Students arrived at the Shule in uniformed dress, girls attired in a black skirt or slacks with a white blouse and an optional red sweater, and boys in black slacks, a white shirt, and an optional red sweater. Occasionally, girls would cover their hair with a scarf or a head wrap and both boys and girls wore black shoes. The mornings began with the gathering of students and staff for the opening assembly, which was held at 8:30 every morning in two locations in the building. The prekindergarten to fifth-grade assembly was held in the Nile Valley Learning Circle room with their school administrator, teachers, and staff. The sixth- to eighth-grade assembly was held in the Pyramid Learning Circle room with their school administrator, teachers, and staff members.

During the assembly, the students stood in a circle formation and took a stance referred to as *angolia*, which is Kiswahili for "attention." In this stance, boys and girls would stand with their arms folded across their chests. Students understood that taking this stance demonstrated respect for their elders and a willingness to hear what was being said. One participant explained *angolia* in this way:

> Angolia is to stand at attention and it is how you have to stand during morning and afternoon assemblies. How you stand when you are greeting one of our Mwalimu [teacher]. How you stand for approval, for the most part you are at rest in between any tabora or a drill, like a tapping society.... I think there was a spiritual element [to it], but also there was a discipline element, because it was about learning how to control and still yourself

from the inside-out. And I think *angolia* in a lot of ways helped you to still oneself from the inside-out. You have to pull from an internal force so that you can control your body [and] you can control your mouth. (Asma, personal communication, 2004)

While standing in *angolia*, students participated in the daily ritual of honoring the ancestors through prayer and libation, the recitation of pledges, and the singing of affirmation songs. They heard announcements and inspirational words during this time. The students recited the pledge, which is referred to as the CIBI pledge:

We are African people struggling for national liberation,

We are preparing leaders and workers to bring about positive change for our people,

We stress the development of our bodies, minds, souls and consciousness,

Our commitment is to self-determination, self-defense and self-respect for our race. (Kamau, personal communication, 2005)

The students sang songs of affirmation; one example is the song, *Watoto Wa Africa (We are children of Africa)*. This song is a call and response, that is, one person says the verse first and then the audience responds by repeating it. This activity, call and response, is a reclamation of traditional African culture (Ani, 1980). A student is selected to lead the song and then employs improvisation as the song progresses. One student related that the song was sung as follows:

Watoto Wa Africa *(call)*
Watoto Wa Africa *(response)*
My name is Kamau *(call)*
His name is Kamau *(response)*
His name is Adofo *(call)*
His name is Adofo *(response)*
(Kamau, personal communication, 2005)

The song would continue in this manner until every student and teacher had been named. Announcements were given, along with encouraging words for the day, and the *wanafunzi* (Kiswahili for "students") all pulled together by saying seven *harambees*. Harambee means "let's all pull together" in Kiswahili; it is performed by the students forming a fist with their left hand, raising their fisted arm in the air and pulling the arm down to the group recitation of seven harambees. Then the students are dismissed from the group assembly and go to their classes.

The curriculum consisted of classes centered in African culture. Studies were designed to present a holistic context for learning about self and heritage and to provide the basis for understanding other peoples (Aisha Shule/W. E. B. Du Bois Preparatory Academy, 2005). Students received instruction from the following categories:

- **CULTURE**—African Studies, Social Studies (History, Civics, Government, Economics) Sociology, Anthropology, Psychology, Philosophy, Fine Arts, Music, and Dance
- **LANGUAGE ARTS & COMMUNICATIONS**—Reading, Writing, Speech, Listening, African and World Literary Studies, Drama, Debate, Oratory, Research/Library Skills, Journalism, Foreign Languages: African and European
- **MATHEMATICS**—Basic Operations, Geometry, African Counting Systems, Business Math, Algebra, Trigonometry, Calculus
- **SCIENCE AND TECHNOLOGY**—Life Science, African Invention and Discovery, Environmental Studies, Chemistry, Physics, Physiology and Anatomy, Research and Scientific Writing, Computer Science
- **PHYSICAL EDUCATION**—Fitness, Games and Sports, Martial Arts, Health and Nutrition (Aisha Shule/W. E. B. Du Bois Preparatory Academy, 2005).

In the Nile Valley Learning Circle classrooms, a visitor might find kindergarten students learning about their identity as African people. One participant of this study explained the importance of students gaining knowledge of their African identity as the foundation of their educational experience:

> They needed to understand [that] they were African children and everything that they needed to do that was going to be good and had needed to be reaffirmed was an African thing. Everything that needed to be in [the] room which was about colors or shapes or styles or letters or numbers were learning about black people. And it could be about black people anywhere in the world but it was going to be about black people. They were going to be inundated and re-inundated with blackness, blackness, blackness and how beautiful and good it was. (Asma, personal communication, 2004)

In the Pyramid Learning Circle classrooms (older students), you might find students receiving instructions for writing a term paper. This term paper would be similar to a college-level paper, with cover sheet, footnotes, and bibliography. It would challenge students to see themselves as leaders of nations, and a comprehensive explication of how they would effect and implement policies for the maintenance of their nation would be expected. One participant described the experience of writing this paper as follows:

> And our assignment was to write…I mean I was so zealous about that assignment, I wrote something like nine pages worth of work. I think the requirement was like four pages, but I wrote something like nine pages. The whole idea was how we foresee ourselves as an independent African nation and what that would be. You know, that's what heads of state do, that's what people who are designing policies and implementing policies that affect entire nations, and the entire world, that's what those kinds of people do. But we were never taught explicitly certainly that…neither implicitly that we did not belong to that group…but we are responsible for re-designing and then implementing new policies, and a new way of thinking, a new way of being, and a new way of teaching, and a new way of living. (Asma, personal communication, 2004)

At midday, students attended lunch at the Shule. The entire school gathered in a common lunch area and one student was selected to lead the group in the giving of thanks for the food. The prayer is recited in Kiswahili but translated into English here:

> One hand to give,
> One hand to receive,
> We give praise to our Creator for healthy food to eat
> To make us stronger.
> To continue our struggle for liberation,
> Justice, and peace.
> We say "Thank you!" (Kamau, personal communication, 2005)

Students ate their meals, abundant in raw vegetables and fruits. The Shule's philosophy was to encourage students and parents to eat nutritious and healthy foods. After the students completed their meals and cleaned up their refuse, they were permitted to go outside for recess. During recess, boys and girls were kept apart and engaged in separate activities. After recess, students went to their afternoon classes.

During the afternoon classes, a visitor would find students in the Nile Valley Circle classrooms learning about the protocol for interacting with adults. One participant related the following:

We [African people] have always been very, very careful [and] deliberate about relationship in role and place. You know children have a place, and it isn't to be beat down and oppressed, but they have a place. As a young adult you have a place; as a full grown adult you have a place; as an elder you have a place. And so we were constantly learning and being molded and shaped in a way in which we understood our place and not that that wasn't an important or special place, but that there were certain ways in which you engaged with an adult. If you were late for class, you had to ask permission to enter the class. If you left the class, you had to ask [to leave], but first of all, you had to apologize for being late and then ask for permission to enter. Anytime a teacher walked into the classroom and at the beginning of class, you stood and you greeted your teacher with respect. You did not leave a class.... You waited for the teacher to dismiss you and then you stood up and you thanked them for providing you with the information and all that you had gained for that day from that class. You didn't just enter [a class], let's say that that teacher had sent you with a note to another Mwalimu (teacher). You didn't just walk into that class, you didn't ever walk through anyone's classroom, depending on where you were and they had open classrooms. No, you ask permission [first]. (Asma, personal communication, 2004)

In the Pyramid Learning Circle classrooms, a visitor might find students learning the third principle of the Nguzo Saba, which is ujima. This principle stands for collective work and responsibility and is understood to mean, "To build and maintain our community together, and make our brother's and sister's problems our problems and to solve them together" (Karenga, 1988, p. 53). A participant of the study described how this principle was affirmed in the students' education:

But it is very interesting about this idea that everybody will take responsibility for each other because, if anybody is misbehaving then everybody gets in trouble. That was how we learned. We had to chant when we would drill "Are you your brother's keeper?" or "Are you your sister's keeper?" and the answer was "No, I am my brother"; "No, I am my sister." Not that there wasn't individual responsibility, but definitely out of that push for individual responsibility came a larger governing responsibility to something bigger than you. I'm always saying it started with you, but it always ultimately went to something that was bigger than you. (Asma, personal communication, 2004)

At the end of the day, students gathered for the closing assembly, where they formed a circle and stood at *angolia*. Once again, the students, teachers, and administrator participated in the recitation of pledges, songs, and inspirational words. In the closing assembly, the afternoon pledge was recited:

I am the first and the Last.
I am the Umoja and Imani.
We pledge to think Black, Speak Black,
Act Black, Buy Black, Pray Black,
Love Black, and Live Black.
We pledge to do black things today,
To ensure us of a Black tomorrow. (Konadu, 2005, p. 169)

This pledge is followed with the singing of the song, *We Have Done Black Things Today*:

We have done Black things today and
We will do Black things again tomorrow.
We have done Black things today and
We will do Black things again tomorrow.
Will you? Yes, I will. Will you? Yes, I will. Will youuuuuu?
One more time (repeat)...
Asante Sana (Thank you very much). (Konadu, 2005, p. 170; Asma, personal communication, 2004).

The seven principles of the Nguzo Saba have been incorporated into a song, and a student leader engaged his fellow students in a call and response rendition. At the end of the song, students pulled together with seven strong harambees. This act of pulling together was interpreted by the students as coming together on one accord and combining their energies and strengths in support of the seven principles of the Nguzo Saba. Following the harambees, the students clapped their hands together seven times. Afterward, the students were dismissed for the day.

Although the Shule was dismissed for the day, many students remained on campus. These students were participating in afterschool programs, such as drum and dance practice or tutoring, and some were just waiting for their parents to pick them up. So a day at the Shule often did not come to an end until well into the evening hours.

In the next chapter, profiles of the participants of this study and their parents are presented. The intent is to put flesh on the sinew of each participant's life, hoping to shed some light into the context of the students' educational experiences as related through their narratives.

6. GLEANING THE MINES FOR TREASURE

It's true that everything has its destiny, but one day that destiny will be realized. So each thing has to transform itself into something better, and to acquire a new destiny, until, someday, the Soul of the World becomes one thing only. (Coelho & Clarke, 1988/1993, p. 105)

As noted earlier, after discovering the Shule, I was able to locate a small sample of participants for this study. These former students graduated from the Shule in 1996 and were members of the first graduating class. They led me to other graduates who agreed with great enthusiasm to be a part of the study. Once I acquired the participants to interview, I decided to include the stories of the parents as a means to triangulate the data collected through the interviews. I believe that the parents' perspectives of life and success were the guiding motivations for exposing their children to this educational model.

In this chapter, I acquaint the reader with the participants in this study and their parents. The objective is to paint a brief portrait of each person to give the reader a sense of who these people are historically, socially, politically, and culturally. The underlying questions that guided the writing of each narrative of the participants and their parents were as follows:

1. Who is this person?
2. What were his or her parental influences while growing up?
3. What was the social, historical, political, and cultural context in which he or she grew up?

An additional question that was posed for the parents in shaping their narratives was this: Why did they select the African-centered school for their child(ren)?

I interviewed one parent for each participant, and in two cases, two children of the same family were interviewed. Refer to the following table for a breakdown of the participants, their parent, graduation year, and gender. To protect the privacy of the participants in the study, a pseudonym has been given to each, their parents, and the school. Some participants were willing to select a pseudonym for themselves; however, for those who left the name selection to me, I was mindful in the choices that I made.

Table 6.1. Participant, Parent, Graduation Year and Gender of Participants.

Participant	Parent	Year Graduated	Male or Female
Kamau	Mama Mariama	1996	M
Heimis	Mama Mariama	2001	M
Naimah	Mama Nefertiti	1996	F
Asma	Mama Busara	1996	F
Nina	Mama Ayo	2001	F
Mumbi	Baba Shombay	2001	F
Adofo	Baba Shombay	2002	M

I wanted to use narratives to give the participants a voice to tell their own stories. Narratives are often employed when attempting to make meaning of particular life experiences (Hatch & Wisniewski, 1995). In the following profiles, I provide a brief narrative of each parent and then a brief narrative of the child or children of each family. The parent's narrative frames the historical, cultural, social, and political context that guided the decision to enroll the participants in an African-centered school. The parent's story broadens the scope of the participant's life, allowing the reader to more fully comprehend the lived experiences of each young person participating in this study.

The majority of the participants, their parents, and the director of the school had names representative of African culture. In selecting pseudonyms for the participants and their parents, I wanted to be mindful of the representation of these participants. Their African names were significant because each name declared a quality, virtue, or characteristic of the person who carried that name (Mbiti, 1970; Tedla, 1995). As researcher, I wanted to respect the naming tradition of African culture, and as I selected pseudonyms for the participants, their parents, and the director of the school, I took care to select a name for each person that reflected a trait or character I observed during the interview process. In this action, I am aware that I shaped the image of my participants to the reader by the pseudonym that I selected, but I am confident that the name speaks specifically to the character of each participant and parent. Also, I use the metaphor of mining as I tell each family's stories. I felt that I was mining for treasure and chose to indicate a particular gem to represent the character of each family.

Mining for Diamonds

- *Mama Mariama, which means "a gift of God" in West Africa (personal communications, 2005)*

Entering into the diamond mines, I found Mama Mariama and her family. They were beautiful diamonds shining brightly in their family love and resiliency. I selected the pseudonym "Mariama" for this parent because I believed it described how her family perceived her life. She and her family had endured a crisis that tested their faith in the Creator and each other. It became apparent as I interviewed her that her children felt that she was, indeed, a precious gift from God.

Mama Mariama has two children who participated in this study, Kamau and Heimis. Mama Mariama and her husband owned a home in a predominantly White suburb about 20 miles outside of a main urban hub, East City. A small population of people of color resided in the area; in fact, the neighbors located immediately to the left of their home were African Americans.

At first glance, observing Mama Mariama in the kitchen, I did not notice the peculiarity of her movements. But later I noticed that at times, her movements were rather jerky and forced. Mama Mariama later told me that she had been completely paralyzed 13 years prior, and doctors did not expect her to ever walk again. However, she was proud of the progress she had made in moving about without assistance.

This family had the ability to make you feel at home. Mama Mariama's 16-year-old daughter, Nawah, assisted her in the kitchen with obvious pleasure. I noticed that each task her mother gave her was met with an attitude of honor and respect. We sat at a table arranged with real chinaware, silverware, napkins, and elegantly arrayed dishes of food, and we prayed before eating. While eating, Mama Mariama told me about her close brush with death back in 1992.

On reflection, Mama Mariama's story demonstrated a critical point in the lives of the family members and underscored the love her children displayed toward her with constant affection through spontaneous hugs and kisses, subtle touches, and playful joking. As I observed the family together, I felt that laughter and giggles were constant companions of this family.

When she was growing up, Mama Mariama asserted that she was comfortable with who she was as a person. She was not an activist nor did she give serious consideration to her African heritage. She offered that her attitude may have been influenced by her socialization in a mostly White school environment at the Catholic school that she attended as a child, but she added that her parents always taught her to be proud of herself as a Black person. She met and married her husband, who was an activist and involved in the Black Nationalist movement. He sought knowledge about African history and identity, and his was the motivation to place their children in an African-centered school.

After her husband located the African-centered school, Mama Mariama went to visit it. Initially, she did not want her children to attend the school. Her first impression of it was that it was "messy" and "it didn't look neat in what I considered a lily white school painted with white walls." Also, she was concerned about her children coming away from this experience without being "well-rounded." "I wanted them to be a well-rounded child like I thought I was...and to get the aspect of all the things that may be more relative to white society." In the vein of being a good wife, she acquiesced to her husband's desires. The event that won her over to accept this educational experience for her children was the first spring program she attended. "These little kids were dancing and reciting poems and telling me about my history and doing things that I never saw done before, and, boy! I was just shocked and amazed how organized they were and the regimen of everything." As a parent, she was required by the school to be involved in her children's education, which meant that she attended parent training sessions in African history and culture. Mama Mariama admitted that she experienced a cultural transformation by being involved with the African-centered school.

Mama Mariama suddenly became critically ill in 1992. This illness was so critical that the doctors did not expect her to live. She was hospitalized for a little over a year. During that time, she was completely paralyzed for six months, suffered from pneumonia for five months, and was bedridden for two and a half years. When this occurred, her oldest child, Kamau, was 12 years old, Heimis was 8 years old, and her daughter, Nawah, was 4 years old. Her husband was so distraught by her illness that he deserted the family, leaving her eldest child, Kamau, in charge of the entire household. She commented that at 12 years old, Kamau "took over two children and a mom and a household…and he still made 4.0 in school." However, the Shule community rallied together and came to her assistance. During Mama Mariama's most critical times, the Shule family became caregivers to her children and also to her. The Shule staff and parents provided care for her children, prepared meals for the family, and even made sure that she was able to keep her medical appointments.

- *Kamau, which means "quiet warrior" in Swahili (personal communications, 2004).*

I chose the pseudonym "Kamau," which means quiet warrior, for this participant because I observed him as a calm, serious, young man during my interview sessions. Yet, as the oldest child of a seriously ill mother, life circumstances enacted a high demand on his young life as he accepted the responsibility of caring for his family through the crisis.

Kamau arranged for the interview to be held at his mother's home. When I arrived, Kamau was in the driveway assisting his 16-year-old sister, who was learning how to parallel park. After exchanging introductions and small talk, Kamau led me into his parents' home, where I was greeted by his parents (mother and stepfather), his grandmother, and his sister. Kamau decided that we should venture outside to conduct the interview while sitting in the gazebo in the backyard.

On first meeting Kamau, I was struck by his serious demeanor, yet he possessed an easy smile. He had a round, boyish face and smooth yet glistening chocolate brown skin. His dark brown eyes were full of life, yet gazing back from them was a man mature beyond his years.

Kamau was born and grew up in the Midwestern metropolitan city. He grew up in a home with his mother and stepfather and two younger siblings. His brother currently attends veterinary school at a historical Black college in the South, and his sister is a senior in a predominantly White high school in a suburban school district. He mentioned that he has an older half brother by his father and maintains a "good relationship" with him.

When describing his family's socioeconomic status, Kamau felt that his family was middle class, and he remarked that, "we were never without." Kamau considered his parents to be African centered, particularly his father, who "was really into African history." It was this that led his father to locate the African-centered school, Faizah Shule, where he and his siblings attended. "He's a visionary-type person....And he heard about this school.... And he wanted his kids to be reared and to know who they are and that is where he sent me."

Initially, Kamau attended a Catholic school from kindergarten through third grade. "My mom always tells the good kids...that school was never a problem [for me].... I always had good grades.... Always A's and B's, I was never a C, D student." Even though, Kamau received excellent grades in the Catholic school, his father's desire that he acquire knowledge in African culture and history motivated him to enroll his son in an African-centered school, the Faizah Shule.

Kamau spoke candidly as he described the school and recalled his many experiences there. He graduated from the Shule in 1996 and immediately enrolled in a predominantly White university within the state to continue his education, majoring in marketing. His desire was to attend a historically Black institution, but he didn't have the financial means to go away to college. He was offered a full scholarship at the predominantly White university, and he accepted it. He joined an African American Greek fraternity and was active in community activities. He graduated with a bachelor's degree in communications and began working for a marketing firm in Freedom City, Michigan. Kamau recently received a job promotion, became engaged, and purchased a house in an affluent suburban community.

• *Heimis, a name he chose for himself (personal communications, 2005).*

"I don't know where it [Heimis Rodriguez] really came from. It came from somebody who used to play beats with Popsicle sticks. That was the thing! I was Heimis Rodriguez and my profession was making beats with popsicle sticks." He explained that he has always offered this name as his A.K.A. (also known as). His best friend went by the name of Rudolph. "And he became Rudolph Adelphia, and that was it. And [we were known] as H & R Block: H for Heimis and R for Rudolph.... We were the H & R Block and it's just been that way since high school."

Heimis graduated from a historically Black university (HBCUs—historically Black colleges and universities) and had been accepted at the HBCU's veterinary school. He knew that his love of animals was a gift from God, and he was determined to fulfill his "calling." Heimis was back in town to visit his family during the middle of the summer. He is different from his brother, gregarious and playful: a jokester.

The interview was held at his mother's house. Heimis emphasized that he was born and raised on the east side of Freedom City. He recalled as a child coming home for lunch, which his father had prepared for him while his mother worked. He felt that his family was a little below middle class. He was the middle child in a household of five people, along with dogs, cats, and fish. Heimis attributed the finding of the Faizah Shule to his father. "I'm pretty sure it was my dad because he was real African centered." Heimis's father was the founder of a local magazine that was African centered, called *Alkebulan Inc.*, and his mother was the editor. Through the magazine, they would bring in renowned African American speakers to Freedom City.

Heimis recounted how he entered the Faizah Shule in prekindergarten. He boasted of being a history maker much like his brother. His brother was in the first graduating classes of the Shule, but Heimis holds the honor of being the first and one of the only students who attended the Shule from prekindergarten through 12th grade. His sister, Nawah also attended Faizah, but she left to attend a predominantly White high school in the suburbs where her mother and stepfather had moved. When he comes back to Freedom City during breaks and vacations, Heimis visits the FS/MGPA to volunteer his services. He believes in giving back to the Shule community.

Mining for Rubies

- *Mama Nefertiti, which is Egyptian for "the beautiful one has arrived" (personal communications, 2005)*

I feel like I entered the ruby mines when I interviewed Mama Nefertiti and her daughter. Rubies are often referred to as a stone of nobility, and Mama Nefertiti reminded me of an African queen. Mama Nefertiti did not adopt an African name nor did she offer a pseudonym to be used for this study. I selected this pseudonym for Mama Nefertiti because, as I observed her during the interview, through her mannerisms and physical carriage, I was reminded of this famous queen of Kemet (Egypt).

At the time of this study, Mama Nefertiti sat on the board of directors for the FS/MGPA and is the mother of Naimah, a participant. Mama Nefertiti is a tall, thin, stately woman who looks younger than her years. Her hair is straight and pulled back away from her face, exposing her high cheekbones.

Mama Nefertiti was born in a small, rural town in Louisiana. She attended school in East City and graduated and attended a major university in South Arbor. She majored in psychology but left college after a few years when she married her husband. They moved to Freedom City, where they started their family. She viewed her family as working class, since she and her husband were both employed at that time. Mama Nefertiti and her husband are the parents of three children, Naimah, Donald, and Charles, and all were enrolled at the Faizah Shule at one time.

Mama Nefertiti does not consider herself to be an activist, per se, nor does she consider herself to be a Black Nationalist or Pan-Africanist. She was not involved in the Black Power or Black Nationalist movements of the 1960s and 1970s. In high school, a teacher "piqued' her interest in African American artists, particularly the writers and poets of the Harlem Renaissance. She did not begin to seek an understanding of herself as an African person until she became involved with the Shule.

Initially, Mama Nefertiti enrolled Naimah in a neighborhood public school. In Naimah's third-grade year, the teachers went on strike for several months. While watching a television special that featured the Faizah Shule, Mama Nefertiti and her husband decided to make an inquiry into the school. "[We] were looking for a good school, but weren't necessarily looking for an African centered school…. We were just looking for a good school," although her husband was leaning more toward the school because of its African-centered focus. They enrolled Naimah into the Faizah Shule with the intent to keep her enrolled there just until the strike was over. As a young, working family, they felt that they could use the tuition money in some other needed capacity. Mama Nefertiti recalled that they "got hooked" and stayed, eventually enrolling all three of their children in the Shule.

She stated that the philosophy of the school emphasized the giftedness of every child, an attractive feature of the school. It was an excellent strategy that provided for the development of each individual child. She discovered her personal development to be a crucial part of the educational experience. As her children were learning Swahili and about African inventors and educators, she was learning also: "I felt that I was learning right along with them." The Shule provided African-centered training to teachers, and this training was made available to parents at no cost. She noted that, "the school had an open door policy, so just through your participation and general parental involvement, you received training of some sort." She was involved in transporting students to political protest activities, local and statewide rallies, and performance events.

When Donald, the oldest son, was in the ninth grade, he asked his mother if he could attend one of the public high schools in Freedom City. He was interested in playing football, and the Marcus Garvey Preparatory Academy did not offer intramural sports. Mama Nefertiti acknowledged that there were several reasons why she seriously considered his request. Her brother had played sports in college and was in the National Basketball Association (NBA), so Donald had strong role models promoting sports. Although her family encouraged her to allow him an opportunity to play sports, she was still hesitant because Donald had not had the experience of attending a public school. She was uncertain of his ability to withstand the influences of that environment. She made him commit to demonstrating his seriousness by maintaining a 4.0 grade point average for his ninth-grade year. She acquiesced and allowed him to go because he had proved that he was serious about utilizing the opportunity to play sports, so she enrolled him in the public school, and his younger brother soon followed.

- *Naimah, a name she chose for herself (personal communications, 2004).*

Naimah opted to give herself a name after a favorite person in her life. She described this important figure as someone who was the director of an African-centered school. She also stated that this person reminded her of Mama Taraji in her commitment to the school and was someone that she wanted to emulate.

Naimah carried herself in a stately manner much like her mother. She walked very erect and exuded confidence. Her complexion was creamy coffee brown and her hair was cut very close, in almost a boyish manner, but yet definitely feminine. She was a tall, thin woman. I recall thinking how a silhouette of her would capture the elegance of her presence.

After a brief discussion about my research, Naimah sat back and began to tell me about her life. She was born in East City, Michigan, and her family moved to Freedom City when she was five years old. Naimah told me that she is the oldest of three siblings, two brothers and a sister: a brother, 19, who was attending college, and a brother, 15, currently in high school. Her father remarried; Naimah had a one-year-old sister.

Naimah began her school experience in a public school. She stated that her parents "weren't really satisfied for reasons I don't know. I was too young. But they found Faizah Shule, and I went there the following year was the third grade." Naimah attended Faizah Shule from the third grade until she graduated in 1996. In the fifth grade, she was double promoted. When asked about her academic performance, she responded, "I always did really, really well in school. Always a top performer, straight A's. I only got one B in my entire school career."

At the time of this study, Naimah resided in Atlanta, Georgia, and was in the process of opening a day care for prekindergarten African American children. She feels that this is a stepping stone to her higher aspiration of opening a literacy institute for African American children. Naimah plans to attend graduate school at Harvard University in the near future.

Mining for the Urim and Thummin

- *Mama Busara, which means "wisdom" in Swahili (personal communications, 2005)*

The Urim and Thummin were the stones of the priests of the tribe of Israel and were used to inquire of God to attain wise counsel. Mama Busara and her family struck me as symbols of wisdom, so I selected the pseudonym for Mama Busara from Swahili that means "wisdom." During the interview, Mama Busara shared a wealth of wisdom on child rearing, family values, and instructional pedagogy.

She is the parent of Asma, another participant in the study. Mama Busara is an administrator at the Faizah Shule. She was a native of Freedom City and had a long history with the Faizah Shule. She came from a long line of educators; in fact, her father's grandfather was a founder of Morehouse College. Her grandfather received a master's degree from Harvard University in the 1920s when W. E. B. DuBois was there. Despite the entrenchment of poverty, her maternal grandmother immersed her mother in the world of dance and the equestrian. She attributes her paternal family with the influence of institutional instruction and attributes her maternal family with the nurturing concepts of the importance of family.

Mama Busara grew up observing her father, a supervisor of social workers and community agents for the Freedom City School District. As a young child, she observed her father, the only African American in his position, negotiate with, appeal to, and even pressure his subordinates in their choices of interactions with the African American and the poor clientele. With unconcealed pride, she remembered, to the amazement of her then young mind, how her father was often disrespected in these encounters, but he consistently responded with fortitude and resolve. If she wanted to spend time with her father, she would often travel with him to his various meetings. "He was gone all the time. Either he was counseling somebody, organizing something, down at the food co-op, organizing to get shoes, taking them to the dentist. He was always on call." She recalled her parents' involvement in community activism, manifested by the frequent hosting of community gatherings in the backyard. Her mother engaged Mama Busara and her sister to listen to the radical voices of the 1960s:

> I remember as a teenager, I remember my mom letting us listen to the "Last Poets." Even though, she didn't like the cursing, she would let us listen to it anyway. She took us to see Bobby Seale when he was here. We had neighbors down the street who were ranking officers of the Black Panther party. So we used to read the Black Panthers's paper and then my father was a community organizer, so we had to deal with issues of poverty, and all that was around me all the time. (personal communication, 2005)

Mama Busara stated that her parents' attitude toward education was that education did not make those who possessed it better people, but rather the value of the education was assessed by the accomplishments that resulted from having it. "What you did and if you didn't do it, what you could [have done] for yourself and community with education, you didn't need to get it at all. What's the point in having it?" For Mama Busara's parents, "[t]he value of education is to make a true contribution to yourself and your family and your people, and if you're not about that then what is the point in getting educated?"

When African American families in her middle-class community were sending their children to Catholic schools, Mama Busara's father resisted the appeals of his daughters to enroll them with their friends. He was a staunch supporter of traditional public schools; his reasons were political. One reason he gave for keeping Mama Busara and her sister in public school was that African Americans had struggled too hard to obtain access to public education to forsake the opportunity to attend public schools. The other reason that he offered for sending his children to public schools was that he wanted to eliminate or diminish the idea of classism. She recalled that he told her, "Now that I make a certain amount of money doesn't mean that I'm going to send you off to some Catholic school…. Why not make it better for all the children instead of just pulling yours out because you have the benefit of money?"

Smiling, Mama Busara reflected on her youthful years of community activism at her high school, when she acquired the nickname "militant midget." She received that name because, "I was so small and I use[d] to have an 'Angela Davis' afro; you know the whole nine yards." Her retort to that nickname was, "Yeah, small but mighty!" As a junior in high school, she organized and participated in a sit-in to protest that girls were not allowed to wear pants or short shorts to school. At that time, school regulation was such that girls could wear only dresses to school.

While in college, her daughter, Asma, was born. She enrolled Asma in a day care center operated by a multicultural group of people and also became involved with the Kiswahili Club, an African-centered organization on campus that brought in guest speakers for Black Studies. She attributed her growth in African consciousness to her involvement with this organization and wanted her daughter to have a similar experience. "I was growing in my African consciousness and I knew for my daughter to have a similar experience and understanding of who she was, she had to be in an environment that embraced that ideology." She felt that cultural knowledge is a critical defense in the struggle of life, particularly within a society that negates the humanity of African people.

Mama Busara eventually enrolled her daughter in the Shule:

> And when I saw how the Shule was interacting with the pre-kindergarten children.... Pre-kindergarten is a preparation for school, but just hearing that language and finding where they taught the children. I really loved that they didn't have the T.V., that they were actively engaging the children in active learning, in active play. That everything that they did had a purpose for some kind of academic or moral or spiritual or some kind of lesson for them to draw from, to profit. But I liked how they engaged the children; I liked the philosophy. The Shule title was "the academy school for gifted children." And I loved the fact that the school embraced the theory that all children are gifted. (personal communication, 2005)

- *Asma, which is Swahili for "higher, more exalted" (personal communications, 2004)*

The pseudonym "Asma" was selected for this participant because I was impressed with the level of insight that she espoused as she explicated her educational philosophy for African American children.

When I interviewed Asma, I was greeted at the door by her and her 2-year-old daughter, Njeri. Njeri was not shy and proved to be an inquisitive toddler. Asma was born in Freedom City and lived with both parents during the first year of her life, after which her parents "broke up and went their separate ways." Both of her parents were initially teachers in the FCSD. She explained that she came from a long line of educators. Her mother, who is a biology and chemistry major, is the fifth generation of teachers in her family, and Asma is the sixth generation, since she had taught kindergarten in an African-centered charter school for several years. Asma's father was a longtime teacher and administrator in the FCSD. Asma's parents met at a local university and were both political activists on campus. Her father taught history and often supplemented his lessons with documents and writings from renowned African American historians, such as Dr. John Henrik Clarke, J. A. Rogers, and others.

Asma was the only child of both of her parents until she was 10 years old, after which she became the sister to two brothers. Her youngest brother attends an African-centered school, although not the Shule, because he experienced some difficulty while there, which warranted his move to a different school. According to Asma, when the Shule became a charter school, it experienced a period of adjustment that involved receiving a different clientele of students and hiring teachers who were inexperienced with the African-centered educational model. This period of instability and adjustment proved deleterious to her brother's learning style. He began to have behavioral problems, and his mother decided it would be best to move him to a more stable environment.

Asma views herself as "different" and believes that her experience with an African-centered educational model has placed her in a small group of unique individuals. She believes that there exist around 20 to 25 African American young adults who have spent the majority of their educational careers within an African-centered educational environment and ideology in Freedom City.

At the time of this study, Asma had married, was expecting her second child, and was a student at Freedom City Law School.

Mining for the Rose Quartz

- *Mama Ayo, which means "joy" in Yoruba (personal communications, 2004):*

Rose quartz is a crystal that forms in the earth. These crystals have been used by ancient and native peoples for their energetic vibrations of love and joy (Brady & Prufer, 1999; Permutt, 2009). Mama Ayo's joy colored our interaction with pure joy and love. I chose this pseudonym for Mama Ayo because I observed joy to be a constant presence in her demeanor as she interacted with her students, her granddaughter, and me.

Mama Ayo was a language arts instructor at the Shule and has been teaching there for the last 14 years. She is the mother of Nina, a participant in this study. I met Mama Ayo on one of my first visits to the Faizah Shule. I observed her in a classroom of seventh graders. Fourteen sixth- and seventh-grade students were engaged in activities within the room, which looked to be about a 10-foot by 12-foot space. In her classroom, chairs with attached desks were arranged in four back-to-back rows. Jazz music flowed from a small stereo system located adjacent to Mama Ayo as she sat at one of the student desks positioned to the far right of the room, and the music softly permeated the room with soothing rhythmic sounds. Upon entering the room and immediately to the right was a wall inset that was decorated with a seven candle kinara surrounded by fruit, nuts, and green foliage plants. Colorful African cloth was draped across the two windows in the room for the dual purposes of blocking out the morning sunlight and painting a visual African culture throughout the room. Several brightly decorated bulletin boards graced the walls; each one announced students' achievements.

My interview with Mama Ayo, however, was in her home in South Arbor, which was located about 40 miles from Freedom City. In South Arbor, Mama Ayo lived with her daughter and grandchild on the campus of a major university. Strikingly beautiful, Mama Ayo had a round face with almond shaped eyes. She had a soft, creamy, coffee complexion and was of medium build. She was adorned in colorful African attire and had wrapped her hair in a matching cloth. Her flowing twisted locks protruded from under the head wrap like branches of a tree in early winter.

Mama Ayo began her life in the South in the midst of a large family of tobacco farmers under the matriarchy of her great-grandmother. She acknowledged that her mother was young and single, and though she knew her biological father, she never had a close relationship with him as she was growing up. Her mother eventually migrated to Freedom City, leaving Mama Ayo in the South with her great-grandmother. Mama Ayo's mother met and married a man in Freedom City and sent for Mama Ayo when she was around 7 years old. She grew up in a working-class home. Her mother was a nurse's assistant and her stepfather worked in the vocation of refrigeration.

Mama Ayo noted that she grew up in an environment in which self-education was very important and she was encouraged to get a "good" education. Although Mama Ayo did not consider her parents to be African centered, she always thought of her mother as a Black woman who actively demonstrated both the pride of being Black and defiance against the constraints of an oppressive society. "I remember her saying that she would never live anywhere where she wasn't wanted…but at the same time, she had this attitude that she could go anywhere she wanted to go…. I can remember us going to the stores and going in the malls and stuff and sometimes we'd be the only Black people there."

While in college, Mama Ayo became actively involved in the Black Power movement. This was around the late 1970s and she noted that the movement had "lost a lot of its luster." Mama Ayo had a strong leaning toward the philosophy of Malcolm X. She did not subscribe to the Civil Rights movement of Dr. Martin Luther King Jr., believing they were pursuing two opposing goals. Concerning Dr. King, she felt "his thing was to change the conditions of our people by integrating and assimilating into America." Whereas, regarding the Black Power Movement and Malcolm X,

> The Black Power movement…the school of thought was that we have to create for ourselves, and we have to be self-sufficient. And yes, we do want civil rights. You know, the law, the rights that are guaranteed to us as citizens of this country but we also are concerned about human rights…not just being able to integrate into the white world but also to be able to defend ourselves if we need to…. Dr. King, his philosophy was a turn the cheek philosophy; non-violence. Malcolm's school of thought was [that] we can defend ourselves, and actually as so-called citizens of this country, that's supposed to be one of our rights, to defend ourselves. (personal communication, 2004).

Also contributing to her growing consciousness and awareness of African culture was her employment as a journalist at two African American media venues, the Freedom City Chronicle and Broadside Press. At the Chronicle, her job was "to report what was going on in the cultural, nationalist community…. So everything that went on in terms of community organizations, theatre, concerts, music, anything that was cultural, particularly dealing with African centeredness, that's what I did while I was there."

Her first encounter with the Faizah Shule was when she was working as a journalist at Broadside Press. Faizah Shule and Broadside Press were housed in the Nat Turner Center. The Nat Turner Center was affiliated with an African-centered church that not only housed the church but also the Faizah Shule, a food co-op, and Broadside Press. Though she was aware of the school and its purpose to educate children from an African-centered perspective, she felt that she could not financially afford to send her children there. She had two children, and her primary concern was to ensure that they received a "good" education, which she felt they were getting from the neighborhood public school they attended. This particular public school had a good reputation and was staffed predominantly with African American teachers. "I was happy that they were getting a good education, even though it wasn't African-centered education."

After Nina was born, Mama Ayo began to utilize the Faizah Shule's afterschool program for her older children, and "in exchange for my two oldest children being in the afterschool program, I went in and volunteered once a week." With assistance from Nina's father, Mama Ayo was able to send Nina to the Shule during her prekindergarten year, but when that assistance ceased, she enrolled Nina in public school. By the time Nina was going into the second grade, Mama Ayo began to work as a teacher's assistant at the Shule. The inconvenience of the conflict between her employment hours and her daughter's school dismissal time influenced Mama Ayo's decision to reenroll Nina at the Shule. As a Shule employee, Mama Ayo was not exempt from paying tuition, but she was able to receive a small discount.

Mama Ayo also related having had a somewhat disheartening experience with the public school system in regard to her eldest daughter. By the time she was in the fifth grade, she encountered her first White teacher who exercised no managerial skills over his class, and her daughter was becoming discouraged with school. She added, "from a nationalist background, our thing is that you cannot turn your children over to the slave master to educate them and expect for them to get a good education.... That's crazy!"

- *Nina, which means "mother" in Swahili (personal communications, 2004):*

Nina was a young mother and I chose this pseudonym for her. She was patient and nurturing to her daughter during the interview session. Even though the interviewing process required Nina's concentration as she recalled her experiences at the Shule, she was never removed from her maternal focus.

Nina stood about 5-foot-1 or 5-foot-2 and was a fair, almost olive complexion African American woman. Nina was dressed in a pink athletic outfit with sneakers. Her reddish brown hair was pulled back into a ponytail. She was born and raised on the east side of Freedom City and attended Faizah Shule most of her life. She went to the Shule for prekindergarten, then she attended a school in east Freedom City for kindergarten and first grade, and was re-enrolled back in the Faizah Shule from the second grade until graduation in

2002. Nina has two brothers and two sisters, but she is not close to her father's children and does not stay in touch with them.

Nina considered her family to be working class, although she had been raised in a single parent home all of her life. Regarding her mother, "I know she was working three jobs and she was, you know, out there hustling everything, you know, so she could do everything for me." Nina felt that she and her mother had a very close relationship, and it was because they were so much alike, plus their birthdays were two weeks apart. "I think us being so much alike helps me to understand her, so I think it helps her to understand me." Nina said that her mother had the greatest influence on her. "She was my first example of how a woman should be." Another reason they spent so much time together was that her mother was her teacher at Faizah Shule from the fourth through the sixth grade and some portions of the eighth and ninth grades.

Nina recalled that she had a good experience when she attended a Freedom City public school. "I can always remember being a good student. I always loved school. Kindergarten…. I was really fortunate to have really good teachers when I went to public school." She spoke about her public school experience:

> We did, I remember all kind of activities and my teacher, my kindergarten teacher was very hands on; she was very involved. Even though we had a large class, she was able to get around to all of us and really be involved. And my 1st grade teacher, Mrs. Lyle, she was like the best teacher. She taught me how to read. And I can remember, I remember wanting to learn how to read. That probably helped of course. We had some bad kids in there who didn't wanta [sic] do anything, but I remember wanting to learn how to read. So that was the big thing. And, but taking the phonics, we did phonics workshops and things like that. (personal communication, 2004)

Nina felt that her grades were pretty good while she attended the Faizah Shule, but she highlighted a few times when she got into trouble. "I clearly remember being the kid that got other people in trouble." Nina was double promoted, which meant she skipped the seventh grade and was promoted to the eighth grade after completing the sixth grade. She felt that eighth grade was her adjustment period. This was the year that she entered high school. She felt that she had to adjust to the transition of being in the oldest student group to becoming one of the youngest students in the high school. But she was able to pull her grades up from a 3.0 grade point average (GPA) in the eighth grade to a 3.4 overall GPA by the time she graduated. In December 2005, Nina graduated with a bachelor's degree from a major university in southern Michigan.

Mining for the Tiger's Eye

- *Baba Shombay, which means "he who walks like a lion" (personal communications, 2005):*

The vibrational tendency of the Tiger's Eye crystal demands that the possessor take action! It is a crystal that represents the character of Baba Shombay. I chose the pseudonym for Baba Shombay, which means "he walks like a lion," because he was a wealth of knowledge on a broad range of topics and I was soon to learn that he was a man of action. He spoke with authority over whatever topic he discussed and could be a shrewd advocator for African-centered education and cultural reclamation.

Baba Shombay is the father of two of the participants in this study, Mumbi and Adofo. At the time of our meeting, Baba Shombay was a tall, thin, African American man. He had a short Afro and his face was clean shaven. He appeared to be comfortably dressed in a multicolored African dashiki and dark slacks. I found that Baba Shombay managed to find humor in his life's experiences and did not hesitate to highlight the learning opportunities his experiences entailed.

Baba Shombay told me that he was born in Freedom City and was raised primarily by a Christian mother. His mother was a teacher in the FCSD and his father was in the Navy. Baba Shombay graduated from a top-ranked high school in the city, received a master mechanic certification from a local career institute, and was employed by a major automotive firm as a technician. This employment opportunity gave him the chance to continue his education, enabling him to become an "engineering technologist." At the time of this study, he was working as a teacher's assistant in the history and science classes at Marcus Garvey Preparatory Academy.

While attending college, Baba Shombay was involved in the reorganization of the Black Students Association. He and fellow students "reorganized the so-called Black Students Association, which always reminded me of the Boy Scouts, and renamed it the Association of Students of African Descent." He became an activist promoting African organizations and African consciousness in the school.

When Baba Shombay became involved with a young woman with a 3-year-old child, he began to give serious consideration to providing a quality education for his children. "[The daughter] was four [years old], time to put her in school. That's when I started having issues with where was I going to put her in school…and Mama Taraji and the Shule was there so that's where we started." After a son and daughter were born and were old enough, he enrolled them in the Shule as well. He was now paying tuition for three children to attend the Shule. The fact that he was paying both tuition and city taxes caused him to become a parent activist in the FCSD. Baba Shombay asserted:

> Now I've got three children in school and the Shule is breaking me. Then that's when I actually started to become actively involved with the [Freedom City] Public Schools, saying that we need to African-ize the public schools because I'm paying taxes for public schools, and I'm paying money for private school, and this is ridiculous. (personal communication, 2005)

As a community activist, Baba Shombay engaged in various activities to engender agency and self-determination in the African American community. He was involved in bringing African American scholars to speak in Freedom City. He also participated in initiating a Freedom City School Board recall. Eventually, he worked actively in the development and implementation of three all-male academies in Freedom City. Once the schools were operating, Baba Shombay, in what he considered a proactive move, enrolled his son, Adofo, in one of the all-male academies.

According to Adofo and Mumbi, Baba Shombay allowed his children to experience traditional public education when they asked his permission to do so. He permitted his eldest child, Gheche, to attend a traditional elementary public school when she requested this of him. In the same manner, he allowed Mumbi to enroll in the same elementary school when she was in the sixth grade and allowed Adofo to attend the ninth grade in a traditional public school setting. Baba Shombay's rationale for allowing his children to attend public school was that "sometimes experience is the best teacher." He felt that they could learn more by actually attending the public school and experiencing the environment than by hearing about the environment. In fact, both Mumbi and Adofo asked to be placed back in the Shule because they felt that the work was too easy and they were not receiving a quality education in the traditional public schools.

- *Mumbi, which means "creator, mother of the universe" in Kikuyu (personal communications, 2005):*

Mumbi has two young children and is a nurturing, caring mother, a role she values. As a result, I chose the pseudonym of Mumbi, which means "creator, mother of the universe," for her.

At the time of our meeting, Mumbi was of medium stature, about 5-foot-5, perhaps a bit shorter. She was a beautiful woman of African descent with a chocolate brown complexion. Her personality was light and hearty, manifesting in her penchant to quickly discover the humor of various aspects of her educational experience as she relayed them to me.

Mumbi recalled that she was born in Freedom City. She feels that her family is African centered, that is, their actions are driven by the question of "how does this benefit African people?" She feels this way because her paternal grandmother owns a cultural center on the east side that operates as a cultural hub within the African American community. Her father is a historian of Africa and African American culture and now teaches at Faizah Shule. Mumbi had just completed a medical assistant certificate program at a local technological institute. She is interested in going back to school for nursing. However, her ultimate desire is to become a child psychologist.

Mumbi attended the Faizah Shule from kindergarten until graduation with one year of interruption. While in the fifth grade, she appealed to her father to let her attend a traditional public school, but once she got there, she found the work too easy and begged her father to send her back to the Shule.

> I went to public school, one year, I think about the fifth or sixth grade. I didn't really like it [laughing]. I had made my daddy put me back in the Shule after the year was over, but the work was just too easy and if in the fifth or sixth grade, I could realize that the work was too easy, I went back to school to get some harder work. (personal communication, 2005)

When talking about her experience at the Shule, Mumbi stressed that the coursework was challenging and the teachers were demanding. She proudly boasts about having to dissect animals for science in the eighth and ninth grades. She told me that her English teacher, Mama Ayo, had prepared her to write research papers. "She had me prepared to do a research paper, as far as the bibliography, works cited page, the body, the content, and outline goes." She said that her GPA was 3.3 when she graduated from the Shule.

Mumbi feels obligated to go back to the Shule and volunteer whenever she is needed. She believes that giving back is a manifestation of reciprocity and fulfills the goal of nation building. Also, she is the mother of two boys and enjoys being a mother.

Adofo, which means "courageous warrior" in Akan (personal communications, 2005)

When asking Adofo to supply me with a pseudonym for this research, he was adamant about using his own name. He felt that his name was serious and "I want people to know who I am basically, even though my name is serious…. And I want people to know that." Adofo's father had named Adofo after a radical African American leader of the 1960s. Baba Shombay made sure that Adofo understood the importance of his name and the history of his name-sake. This presented a struggle for me as researcher. I wanted to give Adofo the opportunity to use his name, but I needed to maintain the commitment of anonymity to the other participants and the school. After much consideration, I decided that it would be best to provide a pseudonym for the study. Adofo means "courageous warrior" and represents my perception of his personality during the interview.

At the time of this study, Adofo was back in Freedom City preparing to continue his educational career at Freedom City Community College (FC2C). Since his graduation in 2002 from the Faizah Shule high school, Adofo had attended an HBCU in Alabama. Several of his peers from the Shule were also attending this university. Adofo was majoring in architecture, but when his funding ran out, he found himself back in Freedom City.

Born in Freedom City in 1984, Adofo grew up with two older sisters and a younger brother. He and his siblings attended the Faizah Shule at various points in their educational careers. Adofo's two older sisters are currently attending a technical institute and both are pursuing medical certifications. Adofo's younger brother is currently enrolled in the Marcus Garvey Preparatory Academy. Adofo considers his family to be middle working class.

Adofo sees his paternal grandmother's and Mama Taraji's work as "a joint venture…because a lot of her [his grandmother's] curriculum [that] she uses and the guidelines for her summer program and our after-school program is based on the Shule." In fact, since his graduation from high school, Adofo has taught chess at his grandmother's center.

Adofo's educational journey was significantly different than the other participants in this study. Initially, when he started school, like his older sisters, he was enrolled in the Faizah Shule. He attended the Shule from kindergarten through the first grade. During that time, his father was actively working with the FCSD in an effort to open several all-male academies. The intent of these academies was to address the crisis of academic failure and specific needs of African American boys. After overcoming challenges, which included litigation by a women's group protesting the exclusion of females, three African-centered academies opened in Freedom City. The particular focus on African American males was the impetus that caused Baba Shombay to pull Adofo out of the Faizah Shule and place him in the academy named after his namesake, Adofo Academy. Adofo attended the academy from the second grade until he graduated from the eighth grade.

In the ninth grade, Adofo attended a traditional public high school, Martin Luther King. While in the public school, Adofo noted that his GPA was terrible. He felt that the size of the school attributed to his poor performance. "Big, too big. King was huge...it was huge. There were one thousand students. They didn't have enough room for the students." Adofo didn't believe that he was receiving a quality education in the public school and asked his father to allow him to go back to the FS/MGPA, and in the 10th grade he enrolled in the Marcus Garvey Preparatory Academy, continuing there until his graduation in 2002.

My search for an understanding of the experiences of an African-centered educational model brought me to these families. I discovered that these families were simple yet shaped in a measure of complexity. The life experiences of the parents were instrumental in creating the rationale for exposing their children to this educational experience out of a desire for a quality education immersed in an African worldview. Yet, it became apparent that once the children tasted this educational model, when faced with the choice, the traditional public education would no longer satisfy their hunger to learn at an optimal level. I venture to say here that the "soul of the world" of these families has set them on a course to co-create this educational experience.

In the next chapter, I utilize the espoused philosophical outcomes of the Shule and the CIBI position statement as a lens to explore the educational experiences of these young people at the Shule. Through an emergent theme analysis, I was able to identify and categorize the outcomes of this educational experience as shared by these former students.

7. HOLDING THE TREASURE TO THE LIGHT

It is we who nourish the Soul of the World, and the world we live in will be either better or worse, depending on whether we become better or worse. And that's where the power of love comes in. Because when we love, we always strive to become better than we are. (Coelho & Clarke, 1988/1993, p. 106)

In *The Alchemist* (Coelho & Clarke, 1988/1993), Santiago has to travel across the desert in a huge caravan to reach Egypt. While in the desert, he decides to stop talking and listen. He learns to hear the language of the desert. It was not the words or conversations with those around him in which he gained his greatest insights, but it was in the stars at night, or the sun during the day, but mostly he learned volumes in the voice of the desert. The desert spoke to him in the silence. Likewise, the voices of these young people are the gems of wisdom that are speaking volumes now. In this chapter, I let their voices reveal the experiences of this educational model.

I must remind you that the collective of families that created the Faizah Shule in the mid-1970s was influenced by the Black Nationalist and Pan-Africanist movements of that time. Joining the CIBI, which operated as a unifying organization for IBIs throughout America, the staff at the Faizah Shule helped to develop and refine the ideology of African-centered education. This ideology that was formalized into a position statement for CIBI was adopted and integrated into the educational philosophy and the purpose statement, which guided the educational process at the Faizah Shule.

The synthesis of the CIBI's position statement, along with FS/MGPA's philosophy and purpose statements, suggest that the educational outcomes should develop young people who undertake the goal of nation building for African people on the African continent and throughout the diaspora. Nation building should reflect in the young person's involvement in positions of leadership, their perpetuation of traditional African culture, spirituality, and in their understanding and acceptance of their roles as adults. These young people would be critical and creative thinkers who are grounded in their African culture and identity. This educational experience located in the centeredness of African worldview systems endeavors to develop young people into "re-Africanized, liberated[,] thinking human beings" (Akoto, 1992, p. 112).

These documents defined the philosophical underpinnings of the FS/MGPA and demonstrated that in addition to academic excellence, the Shule proposed to provide students with the following educational outcomes:

1. An educational experience for young people that is grounded in the concept of nation building.
2. An educational experience for young people that cultivates their cultural knowledge.
3. An educational experience for young people that cultivates the principles of self-advocacy.
4. An educational experience for young people that develops their personhood.

I begin this section with the first outcome, which is nation building. I speak to its importance in this educational experience and then I present the perspectives of the participants on achieving this outcome. I use this structure to present each outcome throughout this chapter.

Educational Experiences Grounded in Nation Building

If it's not about nation building, then it's not about nothing.
—Naimah (personal communications, 2004)

Nation Building

For the African-centered educational model, nation building must be an active process of garnering and developing the resources of African talents for the freeing of African minds and bodies. In this educational model, students are encouraged to reclaim African culture, which is taught and modeled in behaviors, values, traditions, and language. This reclamation is referred to by Akoto (1992) and other Afrocentrists as re-Africanization (Hilliard, 1997; Kambon, 1998). Since education is a cultural act (Hilliard, 1997), African-centered education is about the "reconnection and continuity" of African people (Akoto & Akoto, 2000 p. 72). Akoto and Akoto (2000) agreed that "nation building is an intergenerational process of progressive but intense denuding [Africans] of multi-generational layers of alien values and things, and the progressive adoption and immersion of [Africans] in the culture and the work of rebuilding" (p. 73).

The educational philosophy at the Faizah Shule addresses nation building as the belief that the Shule would provide an educational experience that would "foster in students a spirit of self-reliance and commitment to the rebuilding of our communities and reclaiming our traditional greatness" (Aisha Shule/W. E. B. DuBois Preparatory Academy, 1999, p. 2). The CIBI position statement declares that the African-centered educational model prepares Africans "for self-reliance, nation maintenance and nation management in every regard" (2005, pp. 6–7). Through their experiences, these young people gained an understanding of nation building that is reflected in their narratives.

When speaking of nation building, Kamau identified Mama Taraji as intensely focused on the business of nation building in operating her school. Kamau described Mama Taraji as having an attitude of creating a nation: "Her attitude was [in] developing a nation, a nation of thinkers, a nation of positive people to represent the African Diaspora...all that really means at the end of the day is [that] she was building leaders." (personal communications, 2004)

The concept of nation building for the participants in the study flowed throughout the educational experience when they expressed that nation building was rooted in the individual, the family, and the Shule community. Naimah understood nation building to be the fundamental objective of her educational experience. This ideology was stressed at home as well as in the Shule. Naimah elaborated: "I feel like I was taught that education and everything that I do is about nation building. And if it's not about nation building, it is not about nothing." She said that nation building was "kind of drilled into us." She understood that nation building should be the primary motive for "whatever I pursued in my life." She added that nation building was promoted at home: "My father would…ask me, well, why do you have to go to school? And my answer…would be so that I can help my people." (personal communications, 2004)

One element of the philosophy of the African-centered education at the Faizah Shule was the belief in "preparing talented young people to provide leadership and service for African people at home and abroad" (Aisha Shule/W. E. B. Du Bois Preparatory Academy, 1999, p. 2). Asma recounted a project that had a great impact on her sense of agency and self-determination for African people on the continent and the diaspora:

> I mean I remember one of the assignments that we had…yeah, I'm sure this was in the sixth grade…it was at the end of Chancellor Williams['s] book [*The Destruction of Black Civilization*], and I think that we were talking about a Declaration of Independence or a Constitution…for African people. The whole idea was how we foresee ourselves as an independent African nation and what that would be. You know, that's what heads of state do, that's what people who are designing policies and implementing policies that affects entire nations, and the entire world, that's what those kinds of people do. But we were never taught explicitly certainly that, neither implicitly that we did not belong to that group…but we are responsible for re-designing and then implementing new policies, and a new way of thinking, a new way of being, and a new way of teaching and a new way of living. (personal communications, 2004)

Asma's reflection demonstrates that students were not simply required to think about what nation building entailed but to apply strategies toward nation maintenance and management.

Heimis also perceived nation building as a process that was located within everything that he did, but he noted that the act of nation building first began with him. He defined nation building as follows: "In my mind, nation-building is first, building *your* own nation." He also broadened his definition to include the animals of the earth (demonstrating his desire to be a veterinarian and reflecting the African cultural concept of African people's responsibility to exist in harmony with nature). He further expounded, "I'll help my kids out before I help somebody else's kids out, because that's human nature, but I'm going to help somebody else's kids" (personal communications, 2005).

Heimis also identified simple acts of assisting other African Americans as part of the nation-building concept. For instance, he felt that ensuring that fellow college students were picked up from the airport was an act of nation building. These college students were Shule alumni and had also attended his HBCU:

> Now the thing I do [is] I show love to anybody that's in Alabama and in Atlanta. I pick people up from the airport. That's nation-building in the simplest [form]. Even my boy, [Adofo] when he was at [HBCU], I showed him love. (personal communication, 2005)

Mumbi, a young mother, spoke to the concept of the perpetuation of African people; she perceived the birth of her two children as an act of nation building. She explained nation building as the act of creating leaders from African American children who will have the ability to think critically about their place in the world and how they can be instrumental in assisting African people:

> I'm building a nation! You see, I'm building a nation. How I see it manifested in my life? Well of course, nation-building is way beyond just bringing more children into the world. I guess when you say nation-building, that's the first thing that will pop into your head, having kids or trying to build a nation, bringing more people into the world. It's more than that…that's what the Shule does. Because, they're not having children, they're bringing children. They're collecting children to turn them into nation-builders, to make them think, not about themselves, but about the nation, about African people…. That's the scientific question that we always ask when we do our science fair. Is it good for African people? (personal communications, 2005)

In their descriptions of their educational experiences, some participants viewed nation building as reflected in class projects centered on the perpetuation of the African nation on the continent and in the diaspora. Other participants spoke of nation building as initiating with them first, as manifested in producing children for the nation, and even in assisting other African people in seemingly small ways, such as providing transportation so that they could continue their education.

An African-centered educational experience was built upon family involvement and cooperation within the Shule community, which is essential to nation building.

> *What was really cool was the environment is definitely a family environment…. There is an African proverb that says "it takes a village to raise a child."*
> —Kamau (personal communication, 2004)

Family and Community

The concept of nation building cannot be obtained without the active engagement of the members of the nation-state. The smallest units of the nation-state are individual families and the collection of families make up the nation-state. It is common in traditional African cultures to consider the family the basic unit of the community (Tedla, 1995). However, the concept of family is not confined to the nuclear family as in the Western culture but includes extended family such as aunts, uncles, cousins, and grandparents. This broad concept of family is attributed to Africans' sense of collective importance, that is, that every person in the family is connected to and interested in the welfare of each other. According to Mungazi (1996), traditional Africans understand the concept of family "within the framework of the *oneness of being*" (p. 28). Mungazi explained that the oneness of being operated in the African family from two perspectives. The first perspective was that family ensured the physical welfare of its members, that is, making sure that food, clothing, and shelter were provided. The second perspective was in providing members with a "sense of belonging and an improved self-concept" (p. 29). Within these perspectives, an individual progressively locates his or her space within the family unit as a contributing member.

The aforementioned ideology undergirded the education at Faizah Shule and framed the practice of an African-centered education, which "emphasizes the fundamental relationship between the strength of our families and the strength of our nation" (CIBI, 2005, pp. 6–7). Proponents of African-centered education understood that the family unit is the first and primary unit for the perpetuation of African heritage and culture. When participants were asked the question, "What made their school an African-centered school?" they unanimously agreed that it was the familial environment.

Kamau recalled that it was African tradition and the Shule protocol to refer to the teachers as mama (Kiswahili for mother) and baba (Kiswahili for father). He explained:

> This was my mama, this was my baba, so they are responsible for me like I am their own, and they took that seriously to the hilt. So it was my son, [Kamau], needs to learn. So we were taught like we were their kids...it is like if I was a teacher and I had my own child in school, I [would] want my child to succeed. (personal communication, 2004)

The Faizah Shule also believed that it was important for instructors, parents, and students to develop a strong sense of community through the extended family concept. Kamau noted how he felt that he was fortunate to have been in an environment in which the education of the children was considered a community endeavor:

> What was really cool was the environment is definitely a family environment…. There is an African proverb that says "it takes a village to raise a child." And they made that proverb the truth. It was everybody was involved all of the time. I was fortunate during my time because parents were really involved. (personal communication, 2004)

This view was substantiated by Akoto (1992) when he asserted that, "[effective] parenting within a viable family, which family is also supported within a supportive network of families is a central requirement for the perpetuation of those new African centered values among youth" (p. 35). This supportive network of families constitutes the realization of community for the Shule. Within African cultures, community is the space in which an individual is defined. The community does not exist external to the individual and the individual does not exist external to the community (Mbiti, 1970; Mungazi, 1996; Tedla, 1995). Menkiti (1984) stated, "[I]n the African view, it's the community which defines the person, not some isolated static quality of rationality, will, or memory" (p. 171). Several participants spoke about experiencing the extension of family within the Shule community. Naimah explained her understanding of family as a function of community:

> Based on African centered living and African style of life in which an African—traditional African community pretty much regardless of what nationality you are talking about, what region of the continent you are talking about minus some variation here and there. No individual exists on their own. Family units don't really even exist on their own, it is all a part of the community. So the idea was that we don't have students, we have children and they belong to us, to the community as a whole. (personal communication, 2004)

Another participant, Nina, explained how family at the Shule has become her extended family:

> [T]he African centered perspective is that the school is your family because like you guys said, we spend so much time there. And your teachers are one of the many influences in a student's life and like for us…because our teachers were there and they taught so many grade levels, we spend three and four years with them, so they really get to know us. We really get to know them. And we really get family. I mean, most of my extended family, because it's really just me and my mom; and I don't really keep in touch with my dad's side of the family that often. So my extended family is my Shule family. (personal communication, 2004)

Asma emphasized that her experience of the family environment was not only an extended family environment, but it was also a safe place, particularly when her parents were in the midst of a turbulent divorce:

> We had to refer to our teachers as momma and babba, and so it really felt like a family. I guess the best way I could describe it was that it was an extended family there quite literally. The level of involvement that the teachers had in my personal life, the level of awareness that they had of what was going on when my parents were getting a divorce, I felt comfortable talking with my teachers as mentors. And I felt safe and very comfortable in that because my parents' break up was violent and very hostile. So there were times where we weren't allowed to leave and they protected us. (personal communication, 2004)

Heimis recounted his experience of the family concept as demonstrated by the staff at the Shule when his mother became critically ill. The staff members adopted his family as their own and ensured that he and his siblings had transportation to school:

> [T]he Shule was real family oriented, I give the Shule a one hundred percent credit on being at that time...it takes a whole village to raise a child, family oriented unity, Nguzo Saba. I give them one hundred percent on that. I mean they were willing...especially in my situation where my momma got sick [and] couldn't drive. We had people like Mama [Ayo] use [to] pick us up. We use to get dropped off at the Inner City Cultural center on the East side and she would take us to the Shule because she used to work there early in the mornings. And she would take us all the way over to the Shule. We'd use to ride with Mama [Nozibele], Mama [Busara] would pick us up some time. Heck Mama [Taraji] came and got me a couple of times and that's the principal. She's the top dog. It was really family oriented. (personal communication, 2005)

For the participants in this study, the family and community environment at the Shule was the most salient feature of the educational experience. They recounted how they considered their teachers to be surrogate parents who became their extended families and who offered a safe place, along with needed assistance to families experiencing difficulties and crises.

Another outcome that arose from the data analysis was that the Shule provided students with educational experiences for developing their cultural knowledge and identity. Cultural knowledge and an African identity were cultivated through the students acquiring cultural proficiency, developing a positive self-concept, cultivating a belief in student greatness, and fostering higher order thinking skills.

Educational Experiences for Developing Their Cultural Knowledge and Identity

We learned African culture in the school and we were based on African culture.
—Heimis (personal communication, 2005)

Cultural Proficiency

Proponents of an African-centered education have argued that the struggle for nation building and liberation demands an education that provides African children with knowledge of their African cultural identity. Culture is the meaning-making mechanism of reality for a people, manifested in language, rituals, and symbols. One of the beliefs as posited by the CIBI (2005) position statement is that an African-centered educational practice "emphasizes that African identity is embedded in the continuity of African cultural history" (pp. 6–7) and that history is dynamic and distinct. The FS/MGPA's philosophical statement acknowledges that education for Africans, particularly African Americans, is in the spirit of *sankofa,* which is Kiswahili for "going back and fetch." FS/MGPA believes that African Americans must look back within the African historical continuum to reclaim as well as reconstruct African greatness. Central to accomplishing that mission is the reclamation of the African cultural ethos. FS/MGPA believed that the students must engage in "cultural immersion," that is, students must not only have knowledge of the African culture but essentially live the African culture.

Participants in the study articulated their experience in receiving an education from an African-centered cultural perspective. To them, the experience was essential to their identity development because it was built on their view of history and events from their own epistemology (i.e., method of knowing) and ontology (i.e., essential nature of reality) as an African people. Kambon (1998) contended that these components of a worldview are dependent on a particular racial/cultural experience. Naimah explained her understanding of how the African-centered educational experience enabled her to gain cultural proficiency:

> The fact that this is African and African American history, that the experience of African people across the Diaspora was the basis for everything that we did, everything that we learned, everything was centered around that. And so the curriculum, the core curriculum, didn't suffer because of that but that was just the foundation. So as

we studied math we learned our basic math, algebra, geometry, but I feel like it was enriched by having knowledge and understanding of what these subjects, what these ideas mean to us as African people. Where were African people in 1865, what were they doing? So we had to learn about the Emancipation Proclamation and the formation of America as a country. But we always had to understand what black people were doing at the time; where were people at this time? How did these events affect black people? (personal communication, 2004)

Naimah understood that the foundation for gaining knowledge was in locating African people at the center of that knowledge acquisition. She also noted that African cultural knowledge was imparted to the students. She highlighted learning about Adinkra symbols and learning how to wrap African head wraps. She reminisced that in the African-centered environment, there was always "something culturally reflective." She further explained:

> We learned about the symbols. We learned how the cloth was used, how to wrap the cloth around us, and how to create geles the headpieces, yes. Pretty much in depth in everything that surrounded us was reflective of a piece of Africa. So our teachers, their attire, they didn't have a uniform, but once I became a teacher I understood that they were required to wear African clothes. Not all of the time[,] not even always full African garb, but there should be something culturally reflective, whether it was earrings or a bracelet that children need to see, to see the culture and experience it on a daily basis. (personal communication, 2004)

Heimis felt that the Shule helped him to acquire values through the cultural traditions, rituals, and activities that grounded him and prepared him for his future endeavors. He expounded on this experience even further:

> [A] lot of people say when you have a foundation of yourself, you can go on. Just know who you are. You can learn that kind of any place, but I guess the Shule, it being African-centered...they helped to instill that in you.... I know where I came from and I know where I am going given the values that I've got.... I learned.... But experience at the Shule, I believe help to prepare me for the future more so than the education.... It's not the education of books that grounded me, but it's my experience at the Shule. The things that the Shule did, how they did them, the performances we use to do, the drumming and dancing [that] I was always involved in, my rites-of-passage, the family experience, the mama and the baba, the being responsible for little kids while the teachers are in the meetings, the fact that the school was real little...that whole cycle...helped me be grounded. More so than learning 5 times 5 is 25.... Kind of the fact that I was there was better than the 5 times 5 is 25. (personal communication, 2005)

At the Shule, American holidays were not celebrated; rather, celebratory traditions were established that had cultural relevance. The African-centered concept of self-determination, *kujichagulia,* promoted the ideal that African people create and celebrate their own cultural traditions. During the time of Halloween, the young people in the study reported that they participated in "Ancestors' Day," which represented a time to research and give honor to African family, community, and historical ancestors. Kamau described the significance of that event: "[A]nother thing that we did that was different was Ancestor's Day versus Halloween.... Halloween is more [about] celebrating goblins and ghouls" (personal communications, 2004). Kamau was quick to interject that the Shule administrators never said that they were against Halloween, but "instead of drawing all this attention to jack-o-lanterns and all of these dead, scary things," the students were encouraged: "Let's talk about some dead things that made a difference." Kamau explained that on Ancestors' Day, the students would dress up as an ancestor: "You would become that person for that day. And you had to write a paper on them too.... I am talking about a five page paper...so it was a history lesson." (personal communications, 2004)

Adofo offered another perspective of the cultural celebrations:

Even, they didn't have Christmas but they had Kwanzaa. They didn't have Valentine's Day. It was Black love day. In those days, they did not want to worship a man named Valentine. Who was Valentine? That's the question. If you wanted to celebrate something then you have to know what you're doing. It's Valentine's Day. Who was Valentine? Do you know him? No. St. Patrick's Day, you ever met St. Patrick? No. Ever heard of St. Patrick? No, you just heard of the day. Basically, it's just...Capitalistic holidays. Stuff that'll make you spend your money. (personal communication, 2005)

For cultural nationalists, reclamation of the language is vital to the process of nation building for African people (Asante, 2000; Karenga, 1989). According to Asante (2000), "Language is essentially the control of thought" (p. 41). He argued that African people must control their language if they are to control their future. Participants in the study talked about learning African languages as well as other languages. Heimis's account summarized the experience: "The fact that we spoke Swahili, like almost fluently. So [you] spoke English and Swahili when you went to the Shule" (personal communication, 2005).

For many of the participants, the cultural imperative was emphasized in the home environment as well as the Shule. In fact, in situations where the parents initially were not familiar with African culture, they learned right along with their children. Naimah recalled that her mother and father were also gaining from her experience at the Shule:

I think there were so many things that they had never encountered until I had at-tended the school.... Whether it was just in helping me with homework assignments or participating in school events. And that is still a very important part of the school right now is educating parents.... So there is a lot of education that goes on [so] that the parents actually can reinforce what is going on. (personal communication, 2004)

Upon graduation, most of the participants went off to pursue higher education. Out of the seven participants in this study, four went to a four-year predomi-nantly White institution, two attended an HBCU, and one attended a two-year community college. One can speculate that once these students were not in an environment that reinforced the African-centered worldview, they would ex-perience difficulty maintaining cultural proficiency. When asked how he main-tained his African-centered perspective once he graduated from high school, Adofo indicated that this African cultural orientation had been internalized:

I have no choice. It's there now. It's there now. Subconsciously, it's there. I may not think I'm doing it but it's there. You can do something and not know you're doing it. How I would end up at a HBCU, the best HBCU? I think, it's just subconsciously in there. (personal communication, 2005)

The participants in the study felt that the African-centered educational expe-rience had provided them with knowledge of their historical cultural identity. They attributed this acquisition to their instruction in African history from their own epistemological and ontological perspectives as African people. Participants also noted that their parents were equally transformed through their child's educational experience. Finally, one participant affirmed that once cultural competency was acquired, it was internalized for life.

The FS/MGPA's intent was to create in these young people an awareness of their cultural roots. Yet, they understood that integral to the development of cultural proficiency was the need to cultivate a positive self-concept. Supporting the Shule's rationale for developing positive self-esteem in African American children, Mama Taraji asserted, "because we live in a racist society, that Black children need more intense nurturing" (personal communication, 2004).

We suffer from issues of our esteem, issues around our values, issues around abilities and capacity, issues around black children and academically accelerating, issues around being able to accept that...the three R's for black children are not the fundamentals. They are not fundamentals for any child. They come after the fundamentals which are: who you are, who you are in relationship to the people to whom you belong, and who you are in relationship to the world around you.

—Asma (personal communication, 2004)

Positive Self-Concept

The aforementioned quote from Asma gives a clear description of the difficulties facing African American children in American society. Daily encounters with a hostile and brutal society organized around the ideology of White supremacy (Ani, 1994; Kambon, 1998; Wilson, 1998) translates into suffering from an atrophied self-definition for the majority of African Americans in America. Recognizing and identifying with this experience has positioned the Faizah Shule to strategize ways to ameliorate the often atomized destructions from these encounters. Addressing this reality for African people, the Faizah Shule's educational philosophy states the following:

> Given an educational experience that promotes self-esteem, self-respect, and self-determination, and armed with consciousness based on truth, justice, and service, African descended children can become competent and confident leaders in their communities and in a world of many diverse peoples and cultures. (Aisha Shule/W. E. B. DuBois Preparatory Academy, 1999)

The staff at the FS/MGPA were energized by their belief in the legitimacy of African culture and the greatness of African people. They were intensely committed to the development of leaders for African people and the world. The participants in the study noted the Shule's commitment to this goal; it was not only obvious in their pedagogy but also in their faith and pronounced belief of the "genius" of African children.

Several participants in this study presented descriptions demonstrating their experiences of developing a strong self-concept as a result of attending the Shule. Naimah emphatically stated the following:

> I would not be the person I am if I had not attended [Faizah] Shule. I don't know what would have become of me, but the things that I experienced are so intrinsic to who I am, to what I believe, and what I want to do. (personal communication, 2004)

When speaking of his perception of how the African-centered educational experience cultivated his self-esteem, Kamau elaborated that "it developed a person." He further explained:

> I think because there was…attention [focused on you] and you were taught to drive yourself [that] when I went to [name of university], which was a predominantly white school, I didn't feel less of anything; I felt good[,] happy and proud of being me. So when I went in there my attitude was, hey, you all, how are you doing? I'm here. It taught me how…to be open-minded [and] to not be afraid to learn stuff. A lot of cats [that] I grew

up with in my neighborhood or whatever are still there. They have not left the block because they are afraid.... We went to Africa and we did all kind of stuff. We were out and about. We talked to people who were involved in things and that made us think differently. You weren't afraid to learn new stuff and listen to different music and just a lot of things that a lot of people I find are just afraid to do...I am like, hey, what else can you show me? Teach me something [that] I don't know. (personal communication, 2004)

Asma shared her development of a positive self-esteem. She pointed out that "growing up in a school that's African-centered...you just learn to have a very strong sense of self":

> You always or at least almost always [are] able to maintain your identity regardless of the space, environment, or the venue in which you find yourself. You are who you are in everything and even if you don't own the space entirely, you never lose yourself. You always own yourself. Because you have learned the value of what it means to be who you are where you are. (personal communication, 2004)

Substantiating their perspectives on the development of their self-esteem and preparation for life, some of the participants cited the African-centered education as providing the basis for their ability to go into predominantly White institutions (PWI) and not feel intimidated in that experience but rather feel empowered. They also were not spending their time grappling with their identity while there, a process that they found engaged other African American students. Asma gave her account of feeling grounded in her Africanness:

> I've attended the [name of a major PWI university] as an undergrad, which is very much a white institution, a predominantly white institution and a socially white institution and has been intensely unfriendly to black students until very, very recently.... What was always very interesting to me was how so many of my peers, my contemporaries, who were black [which means] they were young adults of African descent; rather they be from [Westville] which is a 80–85 percent Black city or from somewhere else, who did not have similar experiences [and] who hadn't at the very least grown up in a home which was very much centered culturally, ethically, and spiritually around a politicized black perspective and they've come to the [name of university] to discover themselves...where for me it was an opportunity to be challenged certainly, but to refine my own understanding of who I already knew that I was and to get a chance to kind of play around and learn and discover things about other people...and that's one, the tremendous values of having grown up in a very politicized and very "Pro Black" house, but two, having that constant 360 support in whatever environment that I was in just about my entire life, having gone to the Shule and therefore been involved in...a lot of my extra-curricular activities, particularly performing theater, rites-of-passage were related to the Shule. So just

that constant reaffirmation and confirmation over and over and over again of who I am and what I do and what my purpose is valued and valuable, or really invaluable. I think it made it much easier for me to transition into that institution without losing myself or at least losing much less of myself than I saw a lot of other kids lose…. So I just was constantly reminded of how important that experience was to me being able to maintain things as fundamental as my dignity while I was there. (personal communication, 2004)

Nina felt that her experiences at the Shule helped her become secure in her Africanness, that is, who she is as an African person. With apparent pride, she described her features and accepted the reality of her beauty as an African woman:

And the way I view the world is from such a different perspective…the type of person [that] I am, I'm proud to be Black…. And I'm proud to be African and I'm secure in… the fact, that my hair is nappy and the fact that I'm never [going to] be a size two, no matter how, what I do, how much I diet or anything…. I'm never [going to] be a size two. My nose is big and my lips are bigger…. And it's because of my African-ness." (personal communication, 2004)

Nina felt that she demonstrated more security in her African identity than she observed in other young women who also attended the university:

So I'm a lot more secure in myself as opposed to so many sisters I see come up here to [name of university] who are just, they just get totally turned around. You know, because they come up here and get so bombarded by so much European-ness, whiteness, and you know, so it's grounded me. It's given me a good foundation, and I can come up here, and I can do what I need to do, and I can take these classes, and I can get my degree, but I don't lose myself in the process. And when I feel myself losing myself, I have the tools and the foundation to pull myself back…. I felt I was really prepared for the rest of the world. I was really prepared to come here…. And, from the educational perspective, definitely, I think I was prepared to come here. (personal communication, 2004)

The participants in the study unanimously agreed that the FS/MGPA was committed to the cultivation of their positive self-identity as African people. The educational experiences offered by the Shule were predicated on its intense belief in the historical greatness of African people and in the young people that it instructed.

All day long it was, I want you all to be the best, whatever the best meant. She [Mama Taraji] didn't have a definition for it. It was just be the best at it period.
—Kamau (personal communication, 2004)

Expectations for Greatness

Current research on African American student academic achievement has shown that teacher expectations can have both positive and negative impacts on student achievement (Irvine, 1990; Ladson-Billings, 1994; Thompson, 2002). Daily in urban school settings across the nation, African American students interact with teachers who have low expectations for their academic achievement (Hilliard, 1997).

Through research, African American scholars and educators have deduced that the cultural orientation of African Americans has a greater focus on people and activities, unlike the Western cultural orientation, which is geared toward things (Boykins, 1986; Hale, 1986; Shade, 1994). This orientation toward people stimulates African American children to seek greater positive interaction with their teachers than European American students; in fact, African American students have higher academic success when their relationships with their teachers are warm and supportive (Shade, 1994).

Central to the educational philosophy of the Faizah Shule is the belief that all African American children are gifted. Mama Taraji stated the following:

> Our philosophy has evolved over the years. We have a collective philosophy. Basically, we are saying that we believe that all children are gifted. It is up to the teachers…to identify the particular strengths and talents in each child. And to develop a curriculum just for him alone that will become an equalizing factor for his social and academic growth, for these children. (personal communication, 2004)

This belief in the giftedness of the students was imprinted in the hearts of the school director, her staff, the parents, and the students of Faizah Shule. The participants in this study, specifically those young people who were in the first graduating class, saw themselves as a special group of gifted children who were destined for greatness.

The term *greatness* did not encompass one specific definition, but it was encapsulated in the African historical cultural experience. It was presented in the historical accounts of the great civilization of Kemet. Greatness was presented in the ancestral memory of the accounts of the survivors of the Maafa, the African Holocaust. This greatness was presented in the great works and accomplishments of all the ancestors who have gone before and paved the path for this generation's existence. Young people were constantly told and reminded by the demonstration of invested time, effort, and love of the Shule staff, parents, and community that they were expected to be great. Several young people shared this experience, Asma articulated her feelings succinctly:

But the model of the school was the new African child [who] will have a broader vision, and I think the full name of the school at the time was [Faizah] Shule Academy for Gifted Children. So the whole philosophy was that all children are gifted. And many of us are gifted in different ways. And that's the mission of the school and the instructors were to tap into those gifts no matter how they surfaced or how they manifested themselves for each child. Yes, I was considered gifted among everyone else who I went to school with. (personal communication, 2004)

Asma affirmed that she had never experienced this expectancy for greatness in the public school that she attended briefly:

So our orientation was that…all the expectations were that you are going to do and be great. What you do is expected to be great. Who you are is great already, but we expect you just to fulfill your own capacity. And that was something that I definitely never experienced in a public school setting. (personal communication, 2004)

Kamau, who was in the first graduating class, recalled that "there were seven of us who graduated…it was like we all kind of jelled so well, we were kind of what I call the experiment kids." He felt that because students in his class were the first cohort who had experienced the African-centered education for most of their school career, they were the test case for many innovations. But he and his cohort were also the recipients of high levels of investments of hope and faith through the Shule community. He remembered Mama Taraji's desire for his "success" and also, he recounted the weight of the responsibility that her love and interest placed on him:

And she just wanted you to succeed…looking at it now it was like this lady loved the hell out of us and to this day still does. When she sees me it is like her face lights up and she is like, how is my [Kamau] doing? And for somebody to care about you like that makes a difference. It changes the way that you do things, the way that you feel about things and the way that you interact with people. When people care about you, you treat people like they care about you and like you care about them. (personal communication, 2004)

Each of the participants was grateful for the attention and care of the staff, even to the point of experiencing what was essentially "parent-like fussing" from them. The participants understood that they had become part of an extended family, and the teachers considered them to be one of their own children (Hilliard, 1997). This concept of accepting the students as their own children was a direct reflection of the traditional African culture. The Faizah Shule incorporated the wisdom that "it takes a village to raise a child," and the participants felt that they were recipients of that conviction. In fact, Nina spoke appreciatively about her teacher's concern for her:

So my teachers always...made sure when I got into my slacker mode, they're like, that's not you. Snap out of it. You know, in science class, if I wasn't doing well, Mama [Busara] would be like no, that's unacceptable and I'm not gonna accept it until you do it right. And they always had such expectation of greatness so they always made sure that we produced greatness. (personal communication, 2004)

She further explicated:

So no, the fact that Mama [Busara] cared, and the fact that I went over to her house and spent the night and, you know, I hung out with her kids, and she considered me to be her daughter. You know, really made her invested in my education, and my teachers were invested, and Baba Mwandu, my history teacher was, you know, really invested and really cared about us succeeding. So that definitely, that definitely had a great impact on my education. So I don't know. I just get into these modes, and it's like I don't really feel like doing that and now that I'm older, I push myself because I expect greatness for myself. (personal communication, 2004)

Nina indicated that she had internalized her teachers' expectations for her. Buying into and trusting her teachers' perceptions of her, she began to demand the same level of performance for herself. In traditional African culture, the community is central to the formation of the individual's identity and perception of self (Tedla, 1995).

Fundamental to nation building is creating a generation of leaders capable of instituting self-determination and agency. The participants related how their experiences at the FS/MGPA reflected this goal. They shared how teachers had high expectations for them and were constantly reinforcing those expectations through their investment of time, love, and attention. The participants viewed the teachers like their own parents, often spending time with them and their families outside of the school setting. According to the participants, the teachers believed in them and their abilities for achieving "greatness."

The Shule sought to provide an education that would cultivate the "giftedness" of every African child within the Shule community for the purpose of creating leaders for the African nation. Proponents of an African-centered education believe that critical and creative thinking is a necessary component of the educational experience (Akoto, 1992; Hilliard, 1997; Lee, 1992).

And because I was at this school I was able to look critically at things that were around me.
—Naimah (personal communication, 2004)

Higher Order Thinking

The latest trend in education has been promoting a notion of creating a generation of higher order thinkers (Ennis, 1987). However, the teachers at Faizah Shule have understood that higher order thinking was an essential tool for the reconstruction of the African world.

> Our children's commitment to this struggle and to the culture and ideology can only come through the exercise of their individual thought processes: that is, through the knowledge and discovery of historical truths; through comparison; hypothesizing and testing through debate, trial and application; through analysis and synthesis; through creative and critical thinking; through problem resolution processes; and through final evaluation and decision making. (Akoto, 1992, p. 116)

The Shule's purpose was "to develop strategic thinking based on past and present successes and creative possibilities for the future" (Aisha Shule/W. E. B. DuBois Preparatory Academy, 1999, p. 4). This strategic thinking must proceed from a reciprocal relationship between teacher and students, in which the teacher is student and the students are teachers. This thinking entails examining phenomena utilizing both critical and creative skills. Akoto (1992) asserted that the "objective of creative/critical thinking skills is to equip the student with the ability to be discerning and analytical, but insightful, intuitive and imaginative as well" (p. 161).

One aspect of the African-centered education provided by the Shule was in exposing Eurocentric mythology and the fabrication of "truth" as taught from a Eurocentric worldview and viewing history from an African-centered location (Ani, 1994; Asante, 1991). When Kamau related his experience at the Shule, he shared that history was one of the courses that demanded a critical analysis:

> [T]here were things in European culture from a historical standpoint that are mistruths I am sure in some cases. Like the biggest thing that stands out to me is everybody and their mommas now know that Christopher Columbus did not discover America; why haven't the history books changed? How can you discover a place where there are people? So I think from a historical standpoint we were just...taking different angles at looking at things. (personal communication, 2004)

Kamau further expounded that the teachers, through critical analysis, required a more in-depth examination of African historical events. For instance, in studying the Maafa, Kamau understood that his analysis proceeded from an

African worldview, which is different from a Eurocentric worldview. He offered that the African worldview teaches circular or relational thinking, that
is, "from a cause and effect" perspective; "everything that is old is new." The
"European culture teaches linear thinking.... Do this and do that later and it
just keeps going." Kamau explained:

> Some things are more critical.... And when I talk to all of my other friends who didn't
> attend African-centered schools, they didn't talk about nothing about black folks. And
> what I mean by that...of course, you had your slave trade. Before the slave trade, [those]
> people were doing something. So what were they doing? Let's go and find out...we
> looked more in-depth into that part of it. The European settlers went over and grabbed
> some black folks and brought them here, and they worked for 400 years, and then they
> set them free. Okay...I mean, to hear it like that, it was nothing. Let's look at that some
> more. People got killed. They sank in ships. Four hundred million Africans died, that
> is not lightweight stuff. So it was a more critical look into some things and just more
> expanded horizon of African people. (personal communication, 2004)

Instructions were often given and reinforced through applications. In the
African-centered education, higher order thinking was cultivated by engaging
the students in applications of the knowledge imparted. The teachers understood that students needed to solve problems through identification of those
problems, by gathering important facts, contextualizing, reflecting, and making decisions (Akoto, 1992; Geertsen, 2003). Nina related an experience in
an algebra class. She noted that the teachers designed a project that addressed
the various learning styles of the student, while demanding a critical analysis
of the consequences of particular choices. These lessons were built on the
African cultural emphasis on the interdependency of all things (Tedla, 1995).
Nina explained it this way:

> So just reading it in a book doesn't really help me [to understand] so you know,
> that's a part of the African centered curriculum in the class incorporating things in
> the class...that'll help each child in their particular learning style.... Like she [the
> Mwalimu] had us build this house so that we could apply the things that we were
> learning instead of just arbitrarily looking at them on paper.... So we had to incorpo-
> rate certain angles in the house and do certain things from the algebra class we were
> learning. And we also had to talk about the materials that we'd be using and where
> we would get them from and where we'd build it and what would happen to our en-
> vironment if we put our house there...so not just, oh, I'm [going to] go...clear [these]
> acres and acres of land of all these trees and where all these animals live. What's
> [going to] happen to that environment once I put my house there and what am I
> going to be changing about it and what other life forms am I [going to] be displacing

once I put my house there. And how am I going to be able to live harmoniously because we are the dominant life form but all the other animals have just as much of a
right to live here as.... Everybody else. [T]hat's part of the African centered idea that,
you know, they gave us. It's, yes, we're the dominant life form and you know, we're
thinking beings and we seem to run off more than just instinct. But that doesn't give
us any more right to be here than anything else. (personal communication, 2004)

The acquisition of higher order thinking skills was perceived as a valuable
outcome of the African-centered educational experience. The participants
in the study expressed their experiences in obtaining these skills through projects and frames of reference. The young people stressed the importance of examining phenomena from an African-centered perspective, which is aligned
with their cultural and historical continuum. In this regard, they were also
taught to perceive themselves as the leaders of nations, responsible for maintaining harmony with all of creation.

The Shule provided an educational experience that cultivated the principles of self-advocacy, the third outcome that arose from the data analysis.
Creating leaders for the Shule meant that students needed to understand how
to practice social and political activism as well as student agency.

Educational Experiences That Cultivated
the Principles of Self-Advocacy

*They were training us to be activists from the very beginning, and we always felt empowered
to act and to actually change circumstances.*
—Naimah (personal communication, 2004)

There is no such thing as a *neutral* educational process. Education either func-
tions as an instrument that is used to facilitate the integration of the younger
generation into the logic of the present system and bring about conformity
to it, *or* it becomes "the practice of freedom," the means by which men and
women deal critically and creatively with reality and discover how to participate in the transformation of their world (Shaull, 1970/2003, p. 34).

Activism

Ensuring the goal of nation building requires that the next generation
is actively seeking to establish and maintain the nation-state. The CIBI

position statement clearly asserts that an African-centered education "prepares Africans for self-reliance, nation maintenance, and nation management in every regard" (CIBI, 2005). Also, in the value system of the Nguzo Saba, Nia is the sixth principle, and this principle promotes the concept of collective purpose and responsibility.

While attending the Faizah Shule, the participants spoke of regularly being engaged in activities that developed their confidence in their abilities to affect society and history through activism. Activism (n.d.) is defined as "a policy of taking direct and often militant action to achieve an end, esp[ecially] a political or social one." For the participants, activism was a very key component of their experience. They expressed their memories of going to events and learning that they had the ability to impact society. Naimah's articulation most poignantly denoted the collective experience of the participants:

> But we always had to understand what black people were doing at the time; where were people at this time? How did these events affect black people? I think that probably more than anything else that is what made us an African centered school. We were always looking at current events, what was going on. I always remember writing letters and campaigning to free Nelson Mandela. Whatever was going on in politics we knew about [it]. And we didn't just know about [it] but we were doing something about it however we could at that age…they were training us to be activists from the very beginning and we always felt empowered to act and to actually change circumstances. So when he was freed, we felt like we had done something like we had ownership and we had participated in a way. So in that sense activism was just instilled in us. So I think that's why I feel so committed to serving a cause greater than myself because I feel like I can. (personal communication, 2004)

When asked how many students in her graduating class did she consider to be activists, Naimah responded, "I would say about three out of seven" (personal communication, 2004). This may be an indication that even though all the students were exposed to aspects of activism, not all were perceived as having internalized the ideology of the experiences. On the other hand, participants may practice activism in less obvious ways, such as volunteerism.

Parents also became activists. One reason for this transformation was because they transported the students to the rallies, protest events, marches, and sit-ins that exposed them to the political clout of grassroots efforts. Another reason was that they also were learning how to be activists right along with the children. These events were often not planned in advance, but as the need arose in the community, the Shule was bound by its philosophy of community to meet the call.

Adofo described one event in which students at the Faizah Shule participated in a protest at a major university in Michigan. He stated that "at [name of the university], they had a problem when some students locked themselves in the office as [a form of] protest…. I forgot the actual [reason why], because I was young." When asked if the protest was attributed to affirmative action, he responded:

No, it wasn't affirmative action. It was some students, they were having a problem. One year, they had some students protesting the way the [name of the university] was handling some business. I can't remember actually the situation…. I was going through my rites of passage, too, at the time. I was in 9th grade. And they loaded us on the bus and we went out there and we demonstrated. We drilled and we said pledges and we were basically supporting the people who were boycotting the school. But the people there were looking like these are kids from [Westville] and they're well disciplined. Well disciplined. We were there to support the people…. It was all over the news. (personal communication, 2005)

Adofo continued, explaining that they were transported to the university by the parents through carpools:

It really wasn't anything planned. It was last minute. The students [at the university had] just graduated from the Shule…and they came back [telling of the organized protest]…and then Mama Taraji and other teachers decided that we should go out there. We should be seen, we should show our support…because it was only about five students actually protesting…. And for us to come out there, last minute and show our support, they're like well, it's bigger than the school now. So they got the attention they needed. And when the community sees something that needs to be done, they do it…. You need to see our face, to see we're not playing. (personal communication, 2005)

Adofo also stressed that the Shule supported major candidates with elections within the community. However, for Adofo, activism was not only demonstrated through their political activism but also through social activism that encompassed the community involvement of their performance group, which was the Pyramid Performance Troupe. He described their activities:

We were drumming and dancing all the time. We would go out in Black History month and we play for that all the time. We'd go to every school in [Westville] just about, drum and dance and explain the stories behind African drum and dance. We put on performances all the time at [name of university] State. (personal communication, 2005)

The Shule's philosophy maintained the importance of exposing African American young people to community role models "who were positive and fair and consistent in their behavior," and students were provided with opportunities to be active with their community. Not only were the young people engaged in activism, but they were exposed to role models of activism. Most importantly, when Shule alumni were actively engaged in protest for change, the Shule community was compelled to become a part of that protest through active support and voice.

Student activism was critical to nation building. A key component of "nation maintenance" is producing leadership for the nation and the world. For the Shule, student agency in the form of leadership began within the environment of the Shule community.

> *[The tribunal] just kind of evolved, it just kind of happened. It was like that was the cool thing to take care of your school and be responsible.*
> —Kamau (personal communication, 2004)

Student Agency

Black Nationalism and Pan-African ideologies undergird the educational philosophy at Faizah Shule and permeate the curriculum, the pedagogy, and the activities of the school. Black Nationalism and Pan-African ideologies promote self-determination, self-respect, and self-efficacy for African people. Agency or instrumentality is the energy that accomplishes the goals of this ideology. When sharing their experiences of attending an African-centered school, the participants recollected how they were encouraged to practice student agency. One way in which agency was manifested was in taking responsibility for their learning. Kamau explained how and why he perceived this agency in learning was present:

> Another thing that was interesting was [that] we taught ourselves. And what I mean…there was definitely instruction. Like the principal of the school she taught at Wayne State, and we had straight formal instruction…. But what I mean by we taught ourselves, when I came in [enrolled into the Shule] it was kind of a group [of us] that we all just jelled together and went through this whole thing [the Shule experience]. And the school grew with us…. But we took our education in our own hands. We were always learning, everything was learning. It wasn't like I had to sit [and say] I am in math now. Everything was intertwined and interrelated. (personal communication, 2004)

Another participant pointed out how the director of the Shule would allow the students to select topics of interest for instruction. It was obvious that the curriculum format was not carved in stone, but the students could make requests for various educational experiences and when possible, their requests were fulfilled. For instance, Mumbi shared the following:

We told her [Mama Taraji] what we wanted and when we brought that to her, she made it possible. We had a hip-hop class. We had a chess class, you know, people who just wanted to do extra math. We had extra math. The hardest thing was that we always learned Kiswahili and we brought it to her that we wanted to learn another language like French and Spanish, she made that possible too. (personal communication, 2005)

Several participants in the first graduating class recalled how the impact of converting to a charter school and accepting a different clientele of students was the impetus for executing leadership strategies as they attempted to maintain a modicum of order within the school environment. The senior class formed a tribunal, which was the governing body for the students. Kamau recounted the events: "We put together what was called a tribunal. And it was basically students taking care of students."

[The tribunal] just kind of evolved, it just kind of happened. It was like that was the cool thing to take care of your school and be responsible. It eventually became the higher grades. Before it wasn't an official thing, it just happened. Because everybody was so close we just kind of took responsibility for everything and everybody, naturally. So over time as the school got a little size to it, it was like, hey, this is a good thing. Let's make it something official and it was more. Because it wasn't like you were elected so to speak, it was just a natural progression, you just kind of…stepped into place somehow. And it worked…. It just kind of evolved, it just kind of happened. It was like that was the cool thing to take care of your school and be responsible. Then later on…the school, everybody developed the rites of passage program. And the people who were the leaders of that [rites of passage] became those heads of the tribunal. (Kamau, personal communication, 2004)

When asked if the tribunal made decisions regarding the punishment of students, Kamau responded as follows:

If somebody would do something stupid, we thought of their punishment because it was our school and…just like you wouldn't let anybody into your home act up at your house, you don't let anybody act up at your school…. Fortunately, we didn't have to do it a lot because the attitude was "we ain't having it, don't do that!" In the school the most important thing to you is your peers. What your friends think. We [weren't] having the crap. (personal communication, 2004)

Kamau recalled one particular instance when the tribunal decided that a student should not continue in the school:

In cases where people did do stuff, I mean it came down to a situation and I don't re-member exactly what it was about. But we had to decide whether someone was going to continue to go to the school. And they didn't. Because they didn't want to respect what was going on. They just wanted to rant and rave and be out here all wild. And it's like okay for the greater good of the community of the school and for our envi-ronment you can't continue on, you have got to go. (personal communication, 2004)

When asked if the tribunal had the authority to make decisions independent of the Faizah Shule staff, Kamau explained as follows:

When it came to stuff that big, it wasn't like we could just make that decision and that was it, we had input. It was like we really feel that this person—and people got chances. It wasn't like we said, we don't want him to go to school here no more. Because it was never like someone is un-cool they can't be here. It was some serious allegations of something that was done or whatever. (personal communication, 2004)

The influence of the tribunal became most evident in day-to-day regulations of their peers, particularly with school dress. Kamau related the following: "In uniforms that is when the whole tribunal piece came into effect. You walked around checking people, tuck your shirt in....Tie your shoes up. Don't walk around here all sloppy."

The participants in this study considered the experience at Faizah Shule as fostering student agency to promote self-determination, self-respect, and self-advocacy. These outcomes align with the goals of African-centered educa-tional experience as articulated in the educational philosophy of Faizah Shule.

The fourth outcome that came forth from the data analysis regards the Shule providing an educational experience for young people that developed their personhood. According to traditional African culture, the family and community are responsible for assisting members through life's transitions, which is the process of becoming a person. Fundamental to the evolutionary process of becoming a person is spirituality, the rites of passage, and the acqui-sition of life values.

Educational Experiences That Developed Their Personhood

There is nothing about any traditional African society that comes to mind to me, that isn't or doesn't have a very strong God or Spirit-center, very strong.
—Asma (personal communication, 2004)

Spirituality

The staff of FS/MGPA strongly emphasizes the importance of spirituality in the holistic educational experience of African American young people. The CIBI position statement posits that the African-centered educational experience "acknowledges African spirituality as an essential aspect of our uniqueness as a people and makes it an instrument of our liberation" (2005, pp. 6–7). The ideology of spirituality at the FS/MGPA aligned with CIBI and the concept as put forth by Akoto (1992) in his work *Nationbuilding*:

> Spirituality in the reconstructed and revitalized cosmology of the African nationality must take its impetus and substance from the traditional spiritual formations of Africa…. The essential substance and fundamental assumptions, however, must be at the heart of the spiritual system. Principal among those fundamentals are: everyone has a direct linkage to the creator, each must find his/her own path; our ancestors dwell among us and are available to us; that spiritual awareness; connectedness is a way of life to be celebrated daily in a variety of forms; and the strength of the national collective grows out of its spiritual foundations. (pp. 30–31)

Participants shared how they experienced spirituality in this African-centered environment. Kamau stressed that spirituality was not defined for you by the school, but you were exposed to the concept of respecting the Creator. Kamau explained that when you talk about "spirituality, you are talking about the whole person." He explained that the concept of spirituality at the Shule was not based on a particular organized religion because there were families of many different faiths attending the school:

> [I]t wasn't based in the organized religion; it was about respecting the creator. Part of that is political you don't want to offend people, but at the end of the day that's what it is all about anyway, at least in my thinking, respecting the creator by whatever name you want to call him…. So spirituality was addressed like that because that is part of nurturing the person. But it was never defined for you. (personal communication, 2004)

Ancestor veneration, a ceremony in which the ancestors are remembered for their efforts, struggles, and achievements in setting the stage for those who follow them, is often misunderstood by Western scholars. Africans have been wrongly accused of worshipping their ancestors through these ceremonies. Tedla (1995) explicated, "Africans do not worship their ancestors…since departed relatives are believed to continue to live, they are remembered at numerous events through the act of libation and in prayers for blessings, guidance, and strength" (p. 22). She clarified that this is veneration and not worship.

Kamau gave his understanding of ancestor veneration, which he experienced at the FS/MGPA:

Ancestors were a big part of things. And it wasn't—I have heard a lot of people say, well, you're worshiping dead people. No, it wasn't that. It's showing respect to those who were before you, and that's it. I have seen in my lifetime a lot of people get—and this is where I am different—get really confused with that whole piece. It is like, well, that's false worship and all of that other stuff. It is not about that. Because when my mother passes one day, I am going to sit and think about my momma and all of the things that she did for me, and I am going to talk about it to somebody. And that is all it was. [It is] paying respect to the people who did it before you, the same way when you think about your grandmother. (personal communication, 2004)

Asma explained that the African-centered educational experience had a strong spiritual component. Through this experience, she learned to acknowledge that there was something bigger than she, and this something or someone deserved to be respected as the Creator. She also recognized that her gifts and talents were divinely given and that she should be thankful to God for them. She shared her perspective on spirituality within the African-centered school:

We said praise (prayers) every day before we ate our food. There was a strong spiritual element; you know libations before any activity or ceremony…. [Giving recognition] that there was something even bigger and greater than you. You had a responsibility to pray in your own faith and to be thankful. Which is also something that "faith" is essentially African. There is nothing about any traditional African society that comes to mind to me, that isn't or doesn't have a very strong God or Spirit-center, very strong. Everything comes out of that, if you have a gift, you're intellectual or something in particular, you know that's your purpose. But this purpose is a natural purpose. We don't give birth to ourselves, and think that, you know, we just sort of make up the idea. But it's a process. For me, it's sort of osmosis for us as human beings, I mean, how does our God work? He's organized and planned and purposeful and intelligent and purposed in the way it is meant to work. That's God. (personal communication, 2004)

Heimis shared his thoughts on the concept of spirituality, defining spiritual as being both human and natural. He also noted, in accordance with African thoughts on spirituality, that humans are not separate entities of spirit. Traditional African religion believes that humans are body, soul, and spirit united. Heimis explained further:

Spirituality is fun. Spirituality is human, nature. I don't care what you believe in…. I don't think it is a separate entity. We're not separate entities, we're not…. I'm not [Heimis] and then spiritual [Heimis]. I'm [Heimis] right here talking to you from body, mind and soul. That's who I am. I'm all; I'm all at that moment. Just like the Father, Son and Holy Spirit as one team, with three aspects but one team. I'm one thing and that's how life is, you don't go to school as a person and then go home as a spirit. You don't, I mean, I'm adult so I can talk about it, you don't have sex as a human body and then have a spirit. You're a spirit in a human body having sex and that's what you are and then that's taught. We are not beings with separate parts. (personal communication, 2005)

He also demonstrated his understanding of the potency of African spirituality as a legacy of African resiliency:

We had to be spiritual to take crap from a whip; you had to be spiritual if your daddy is hanging from a tree, that forbidden fruit. You have to be, you know…. So that's just the way I feel. (personal communication, 2005)

Adofo shared his experience with spirituality through both the FS/MGPA and the influence of his parents:

Well, if you go to ancient Africa, their religion is spiritual. The things they did were spiritual. The gods, the kings, the rulers who ruled were viewed as gods. People were very spiritual, like incense. Everything has meaning. My mom is a very spiritual person…. My father [believes that] certain incense, certain oils brings [sic] certain vibes. And certain vibes you let off are how people, how people deal with you. And being spiritual…my parents believe that there's always someone looking over you. [If] my father had a bad day, he'd say I must've disappointed the ancestors. [If] my father had a good day, the ancestors are looking out for me. The ancestors [have] been good. He calls them ancestors…. That goes back to ancient Africa. (personal communication, 2005)

The participants in the study recognized the importance of spirituality within the framework of the African-centered education. They articulated the necessity of acknowledging the Creator as a power greater than themselves. It seemed apparent that the emphasis on spirituality within the FS/MGPA was an extension of the significance of spirituality within the home environments. As they expressed their experiences on spirituality, the young people infused their narratives with indicators of their parents' religious influence.

For Africans, spirituality is the essence of human existence within the material world. African cosmology maintains that spirits enter the material world as babies and through family and community are developed into personhood. This human development is acknowledged and advanced through rituals, ceremonies, and celebrations of transitions of life called rites of passage. The Shule understood the importance of life's transitions and incorporated the rites of passage into their students' educational experience.

Well, rites-of-passage is...a basic meaning from my understanding...it's not really a rites-of-passage of the body, it's really of the mind.

—Heimis (personal communication, 2005)

Rites of Passage

According to the CIBI's (2005) position statement, one objective of an African-centered education is to

> ensure that the historic role and function of the customs, traditions, rituals, and ceremonies—that have protected and preserved our culture; facilitated our spiritual expression; ensured harmony in our social relations; prepared our people to meet their responsibilities as adult members of our culture; and sustained the continuity of African life over successive generations—are understood and made relevant to the challenges that confront us in our time. (pp. 6–7)

In accordance with this statement, the Shule believes that young people must be taught their roles in society for the reclamation and restructuring of African greatness, and the Shule community has a responsibility to impart that knowledge to the students. One vehicle that the Shule has utilized to integrate this ideology into the educational experience of its students has been through the rites-of-passage program.

Participants in this study described their rites-of-passage experience. They spoke of experiencing two rites-of-passage ceremonies during their educational career at the FS/MGPA. The first rites-of-passage program was experienced around the eighth grade and was considered by the young people to be the adult rites. The second rites-of-passage program was around the ages of 14 to 16 and was called the Baba or Mama rites. Drawing on and adapting the traditions of African cultural rituals, the teachers, parents, and community members created a rites-of-passage program specific to the needs of these young men and women.

According to the participants, the first rite of passage was a weeklong experience for both the male and female students, separately. Naimah provided an overview of the first rites-of-passage program for the girls:

> The rites of passage program [was performed] when we were 12 and [when] we were about to graduate [from high school], there were certain rituals and procedures that were integrated into our curriculum as well as after school programs, as well as assignments and tasks that we had to perform at home with our mothers at the time, for the

girls it was our mothers. So whether it was an assignment in terms of keeping our rooms clean or interviewing an elder in our family, the assignment that was going on at school, it related directly to what was going on at home. (personal communication, 2005)

According to the participants, entering into puberty was not a precursor to this experience; it was simply an experience that you had when the elders (older women) felt that you were ready. Nina explained this process: "So when you get to the prep school, you go through your first rites…and it's supposed to bring you into young womanhood…and the mamas start to… cultivate the woman in you, instead of the little girl…if they feel that you're ready" (personal communication, 2004).

Heimis recounted his thoughts on the rites-of-passage experience: "People tend to think it's dealing with the body when you're going through puberty and things like that, but one thing the Shule always reflected upon was when you were mentally ready" (personal communication, 2005). He mentioned that some students had been dropped from the rites-of-passage lines if they were perceived as not being mentally ready to go through the experience:

It's the transformation from boyhood to manhood. You don't do rites-of-passage over…though it might be a six month passage or a two month passage…it is preparation for manhood…. in the rites-of-passage, you've got to be taught that there are consequences for everything. And that there are things that you do now that leads up to what will happen to you later. (personal communication, 2005)

Heimis further stated that this experience was really about resocialization: "It's a re-socialization indeed. In fact, [that's] one of the biggest parts of it; it is big because we learn through socialization…. Oh yea, it's a re-socialization…. It's a re-thinking" (personal communication, 2005). Heimis stated that during the rites-of-passage program, the young men were involved in both physical and mental activities.

When the rites-of-passage program was first developed, it was not very elaborate; the initiation usually only lasted a week. However, as the program continued through the years, it was refined and elaborated into several months. Naimah acknowledged that, "as the years went on, it became much more sophisticated and…the preparation for the rites-of-passage starts months, months ahead of time" (personal communication, 2004). Although both males and females reported experiencing two rites of passage, the second, which took place during high school, was articulated on with greater frequency by both groups of participants.

During the latter rites-of-passage program, the males and females experienced this ritual in some very different ways. The males experienced separation from the community by being taken on a field trip for wilderness training. The male elders, consisting of teachers, parents, and community persons, prepared and accompanied the young men, who were between the ages of 14 and 17, on a "camping" trip. At this gathering, which lasted for a week, the students were taken through a rigorous program of values impartation, strength training, relationship building, bonding, and explication of the expectations and objectives of manhood (i.e., sexuality, fatherhood, and being a provider and community leader).

Female students experienced a symbolic seclusion. In most cases, the young women were not taken on retreats away from the community but were required to participate in a "communication fast." They were restricted from speaking with their fathers and brothers during this time. Their time was spent in the presence of their mothers and female elders where they received instructions, were counseled, and were assigned tasks. As the program evolved and became "more sophisticated," according to Naimah (personal communication, 2004), female participants engaged in hiking trips and formed drill teams to establish discipline.

Both male and female participants were explicit about the lessons learned through their rites-of-passage experiences. Asma expressed that through this experience, she was able to link her role and place in the genesis of civilization, which is often negated in the European ethos. She also pointed out that the rites-of-passage experience was instrumental in understanding her womanhood and sexuality. While attending a major university, she noticed that young African American women were allowing themselves to be exploited as they attempted to enter into and maintain relationships with a scarce supply of African American men. Asma adamantly refused to get caught up in that game and explained that her attitude was shaped by her rites-of-passage experience: "To a large extent….it's how you think about desire, yourself as a woman, and as an African American woman." She further expounded: "You know, we heard a lot about being the mother of civilization, coveting the Black woman's womb, everything that exists in the universe exists inside of you. Your womb is a microcosm for the entire universe." She affirmed that the rites-of-passage experience helped her to perceive herself as valuable, and she resolved not to allow herself to be exploited.

Kamau and his brother, Heimis, revealed that while going through their rites-of-passage program, they were the leaders of their groups. The young men were initiated into the Akoben Sankofa Warrior Society and were considered to be young warriors. In this group, they learned "the responsibilities of being a warrior," and Heimis continued, "You learn the responsibilities that a man is generally supposed to have to at least be able to survive" (personal communication, 2005). Kamau added that the experience of accepting and operating as a leader in the rites-of-passage group led to initiating leadership in the formulation of a student tribunal to regulate and govern student behavior.

When asked if understanding sexuality was a part of the rites-of-passage training, Heimis acknowledged that they were instructed about their sexuality: "You make sure you understand the consequences, the responsibilities of what happens, statistically why it happens, when and where.... You keep going with it, and you have rap sessions about it" (personal communication, 2005).

Part of the rites-of-passage program is to teach young people the importance of community. The participants spoke about the ways the program enables students to bond together as a community. Nina shared how part of the program was to teach young women to appreciate other young women. In Western culture, women tend to objectify each other and view other women as threats (hooks, 1993). Nina explained:

> So often when we get to a certain point, it's like women become our enemies, and it's about trying to dispel that and make us accept one another as our friends.... Because we share some experiences, so women shouldn't be your enemies...so they want us to be strong women; they want us to be sisters. (personal communication, 2004)

Heimis highlighted this effort of bonding and appreciating the collective also:

> For those [that] I went through [the rites-of-passage with] ranged like from, I believe the youngest one I'm sure, from 14 to about 17 [years old]. Then again, that number gives you a broad spectrum of people, different minds, different angles of thinking... and it is sorta like a family. It builds a sense of unity because this is one group. All different walks of life, different shades, different growth, different financial everything and you become on one accord. Then you have a line, a line of brothers who are supposed to be in sync. (personal communication, 2005)

Once the participants have successfully completed the program, a celebration is held in their honor, separately for males and females. Same-sex family members, teachers, staff, and elders in the community gather in ceremony to celebrate the incorporation of the person into the community. It announces the symbolic resurrection of the participant as a new person, an adult who now has all the privileges and responsibilities bestowed on adulthood. In the Baba and Mama rites-of-passage, this person is now referred to as Mama or Baba and is respected as such.

Overall, the participants described their rites-of-passage experience as a positive event in their lives. All of them clearly articulated the objective of the program as a transformative event in which they would enter as a child and emerge from as an adult. However, in this study, some of the male participants seemed skeptical as to the mystical powers of the transformation into manhood. Kamau opined that "rites-of-passage was just a formalized situation…of showing young men and young women what being responsible and being adults is…. True rites-of-passage is growing up, period!" (personal communication, 2004).

Keeping in line with the concept of nation building and the cultural focus of the FS/MGPA, the rites-of-passage program provided the venue to pass on the customs, traditions, rituals, and ceremonies to African American young people. The goal of this cultural impartation is to transform nonpersons into persons and to incorporate them into the Pan-African community in an effort to maintain and perpetuate the liberation of African people on the continent and the diaspora.

In the development of personhood through the rites-of-passage program and the African-centered educational experience, life values are imparted to the students. The values of the Nguzo Saba and Maat are integrated into the educational experiences of the students; often they were not specifically articulated but were modeled through daily interactions and rituals:

> And sometimes when people hear Nguzo Saba they hear certain things; they think of these very constructed definitions…. But it's so much more than that, especially when you accept them into your life and into the basis for the way that you live.
> —Nina (personal communication, 2004)

Life Values

In traditional African culture, the goal of education is social, with a mission of developing personhood. The family and community, collectively, imparts values to its members to facilitate the development of virtue and character in persons who will perpetuate righteousness, harmony, truth, justice, order, reciprocity, and balance. This process of education is lifelong because a person is considered to always be in the process of becoming a person. In the community of the Faizah Shule, the Nguzo Saba and the principles of Maat are incorporated into the day-to-day human interactions within the school environment. The seven principles of the Nguzo Saba are recited in song at the end of each day, and oftentimes, monthly "themes" based on these principles are taught.

The participants were intensely aware of the principles of life that guided their human interactions with members of the community. These principles were so internalized that the participants, although mentioning the system of values, often did not compartmentalize the values into separate parts but spoke of them holistically. They understood them to be so interrelated and interwoven. These principles were fundamental to their life choices. Participants cited how values learned from their educational experience at the African-centered school were manifested in their lives, particularly once they left the environment.

Several of the participants graduated from the Shule and began their pursuit of higher education at predominantly White institutions. The following are accounts of their experience at the higher education institution and the impact of their African-centered education on that experience. Naimah asserted that because of her experience at the Shule, she entered the university expecting to take on a leadership role:

> So when I went to the [name of university], it was my duty to assume a position of leadership[,] whether that be through the Black Student Union or to create another organization that was geared toward African American women, Caucus of the Sisters. It was just somebody has got do it, and I have got to be the one to step up to the plate or it won't get done. And if it does get done, it's not going to get done right. So I just have to do it myself. (personal communication, 2004)

While attending a predominantly White institution, Kamau decided that he would pledge a Black Greek Fraternity. To some, including myself, this may seem initially to be a contradiction of African-centered values. Kamau presented the following rationale for joining the fraternity. First, he attributed his educational experience at the Shule with influencing that decision:

> Yes, [the Shule influenced this decision] when you think about it from a nation-building standpoint.... For one it was about brotherhood, about positivity. It was about connecting, not so much networking, but literally connecting with a band of people that are together for a reason. So from an Afrocentric standpoint, I think that's where that came into play. (personal communication, 2004)

Kamau recognized that joining a Greek fraternity raised issues in the minds of some proponents of African-centered thought:

> On the flipside of that a lot of African-centered people, quote unquote, had a problem with it. Like why do you want to join a Greek—da? And that's where again, that whole thing of wearing it on your sleeve versus it being internal, [that's] what you are…that's where those things differ…if you thought about it, African American people got together and formed these organizations the same way that the school came together. It was unifying us and it was keeping something that we can hold on to that's ours, gives us identity and bonding together as one. That's what that was about. It just happened to be named with Greek letters because we didn't have [anything] else. It wasn't—I am not a Greek organizations [sic], don't talk nothing about being Greek. We just got Greek letters as the name. If you said it in Swahili would that help you? Would that make it Afrocentric for you? Mama [Taraji] always said and this always stuck with me is that we are a new African people; she said that all of the time. We are a new African people. (personal communication, 2004)

Asma perceived an African-centered education as a lifestyle, not just a teaching strategy. She spoke of the ways values were imparted within the students at Faizah Shule, and she considered the Nguzo Saba an appropriate values system for imparting virtue and character. She gave an account of the values impartation:

> African centered education is not a way of teaching; it is a way of life…. The way you think…the way you breathe. It is a way in which you engage the world, the way in which you think about yourself and how you apply that conception to your children…. As a child carrying that idea into adulthood is the sort of thing that I was talking about, just being able to maintain my basic dignity. Because being respected and being respectable was more important to me than being popular. (personal communication, 2004)

Asma offered more insight into the internalization of the values at Faizah Shule:

> One of the really wonderful dynamics about the Shule was that it was very firmly rooted in principle, and the principles utilize the Nguzo Saba. A lot of people like to associate that with Kwanzaa, at a particular time of the year, particular days…really we were taught to perceive that these were the seven principles that Blackness actually founded on the Nguzo Saba…so we learn Nguzo Saba, it wasn't just umoja-unity, kujichagulia focus on me and myself…kujichagulia: define ourselves, speak for ourselves, create for ourselves rather than being named, defined and spoken for by others as Maulana Karenga has both outlined and designed in a much more comprehensive

way. So Kuumba to leave our environment more beautiful and beneficial than we inherited it, that's what we are responsible for doing. So when we were walking around in our black sole shoes and scuffing up the floor…in morning assembly, we had to stand in "Angola," [a position of readiness] which was about discipline…. We might be standing there for a half hour in Angola and you better not [talk] while Mama [Taraji] is talking. And there is still something about that woman's voice that just sort of calls you to attention. But very much like a mother[,] "What are you children doing leaving these scuff marks all over the floor?" So we had to go around in a very simple motion where we had to use the bottom of our shoes, so it wouldn't scuff up some more. What we couldn't get up, she wouldn't fret about the few that were left. But it was like, they took complete ownership of everything relating to us. (personal communication, 2004)

Asma continued to expound on one of the values of Nguzo Saba, which enforces the concept of collectivity and taking on your brother's problems as your own. Ujima, collective work and responsibility, is the principle of Nguzo Saba, emanating from the concept of community:

But it is very interesting about this idea that everybody will take responsibility for each other because if anybody is misbehaving than [sic] everybody gets in trouble. That was how we learned. We had to chant when we would drill[,] "Are you your brother's keeper?" or "Are you your sister's keeper?" and the answer was[,] "No, I am my brother," "No, I am my sister." Not that there wasn't individual responsibility, but definitely out of that push for individual responsibility came a larger governing responsibility to something bigger than you. I'm always saying it started with you, but it always ultimately went to something that was bigger than you. (personal communication, 2004)

Heimis did not view this principle favorably. He indicated that he understood the underlying value of unity the principle promotes, but at the same time, he felt that the principle was taken to the extreme when everyone suffered the consequences of the actions of one or two. He offered his perspective:

Promoting unity is the [African] centered thing. Something they used to do. If one person did [it], everybody did it and that brings the group together and makes sure you're whole. And the premise was to teach you to keep your brothers in line…your boy…pull his coat tail. That's excellent! That's exceptional…but at the same token, if somebody don't do something and everybody gets sent home for it, you can keep that! (personal communication, 2005)

Nina, another participant, provided her understanding of how her actions directly impacted others:

I know that my actions have such a great impact on people. There are people that I
know who are [going] to be directly affected by it but also people who are going to be
affected by it just from the residual effects. If I make a mistake and I do something and
my mom has to...say for example, she has to take [Habibah] to the Shule and it makes
her late for work. That throws off what's going on at the Shule. That throws off their
day and it throws off some of the students. The students can't get done. So I'm just
saying that every action has a reaction and that's something that we're really forced
to look at and really understand because you can't just go around in the world and decide that you're [going to] do something and expect there not to be a consequence for
it. So, it's stuff like that that I picked up from the Shule that has really impacted the
way that I live my life and the way that I view the world. Even some of the things in
the world that's going on right now, this whole war thing, I don't feel like anybody's
really looking at the impact that it's having on the people who live in these countries
that these armies are just going in and bombing. What about these children and what
about these people? (personal communication, 2004)

Mumbi explained how the Nguzo Saba principle of ujima has been carried
over in the rearing of her children. She hypothesized an incident in which
her son, who is 3 years old, would have a friend come over to play. Before
the friend could leave to go home, Mumbi explained that she would have
him assist her son in cleaning up the play area. Speaking of her son, Mumbi
explicated, "Sometimes he might have company, I would tell his friends to
clean up. They're not going to leave my son with all this mess. They're little,
but they help [to] make the mess. His friend is going to help clean it up also"
(personal communication, 2005).

Several of the participants in the school were young mothers. Contrary to
Western culture, where a fetus is not considered to be a person, and a pregnant
woman has the legislative right to choose whether to give birth, traditional
African culture promotes a different orientation toward life and what is considered the origins of life. Traditional African culture promotes the belief that
a fetus is a person, specifically, a returning ancestor into the earth realm. That
life is welcomed and honored into the community prior to birth (Mbiti, 1970).

In the rites-of-passage program, the young women in this study were
taught about their sexuality and motherhood responsibilities, as well as their
roles within the community. When these young women became pregnant,
they made the choice to give birth and raise their child. Pregnancy for them
did not mean that they had made a mistake and now were experiencing an unwanted pregnancy but rather that the Creator had given them a gift. Mumbi
shared her account of how her understanding of African culture regarding
children helped her decide what to do about her pregnancy:

Once you find out you're pregnant, that's a live child. That's a live human being. That's a person! That's African culture…that's a person. Now you might did it out of wedlock [or] you might not, but it's still a person, so you keeping that person because this person can do something that you won't do, and it could be a better person than you or anybody else. It is a person. That is the first thing that comes to my mind with him, that he could be and do anything, and I wouldn't try to discourage him or make him try to be something that I want him to be. I want him to be exactly who he is and what he wants to be. Well, the African culture always encourages you to have children and make more babies, so our culture won't die. Like now, they like to call us the minority, but we are the majority and I tell you, we like to have kids. Can't help it! It's almost like it's part of us to be nurturers, to be mothers. (personal communication, 2005)

Regarding her pregnancy, she acknowledged that her child wasn't planned, "but once I found out I was pregnant, it was nothing nobody was going to tell me" (personal communication, 2005). Mumbi was optimistic about her future; she didn't see why her life had to stop because of her pregnancy. In fact, she planned to go on to college. She gave a glimpse into her thoughts at the time:

I did good at high school. I didn't slack; I wasn't bad, I didn't run away from home, I wasn't that type of person. I'm not a statistic, because most girls get pregnant in high school when they are 16. I didn't even start having sex until I was 18. So when I found out I was pregnant, I said "Oh, I'm starting school." People tried to talk me out of it. They kept trying to discourage me. I'm not trying to hear that, just because I'm having a baby doesn't mean that my whole life has got to stop. When I got pregnant with him, it wasn't on purpose. I didn't say, like, oh yeah, I'm about to get pregnant, but I knew that was a possibility. So when it happened, it was just like, okay. Got me a baby! (personal communication, 2005)

Nina, also a young mother, recounted her experience once she found out she was pregnant and the impact of her African-centered education on her decision to have the baby. Although she indicated that she had issues with becoming pregnant so young, she relied on her values learned from attending the Shule: "Children are always welcomed." The following is her account:

So you know, it [African centered education] has given us a foundation to be secure African people, in my case, secure African woman. I mean, having a baby out of wedlock and I was so young. I got pregnant at seventeen. But even though I have my issues with it and stuff like that, in my heart I knew it was going to be okay. Children are always welcomed. You know, children are always a blessing. So you know, that's the way I was raised in African-centered space, children are always a blessing. (personal communication, 2004)

Becoming pregnant so young was not without negative experiences and unsolicited physician advice. Asma shared the following:

> I faced ridicule because I have a baby so young and I wasn't married and I had to finish school. The doctor that I went to, a white lady, actually advised me to get an abortion and it wasn't like discussing my options. It was like, if I were you, if you were my daughter, if I was in this situation, this is what I would do, and that's the best thing. (personal communication, 2004)

Asma acknowledged that the experience was difficult, but she had the support of her mother to help her through it. Her mother even moved in with her on campus so that she could provide child care while Nina completed her higher education program. Nina spoke of the difficult experience and her mother's support:

> It has been hard, you know what I'm saying, having a child and trying to finish school and stuff like that, but my mom's supported me and my family has backed me up and, you know, she [her daughter] goes to the Shule some days. You know, my mama has the freedom, like she takes her to daycare, but if she can't take her to daycare, then she just takes her to Shule, where she runs around with the kids and goes to Mama [name] classroom. It has given me a strong foundation and the world is so much different. Just that one thing, I know that she's a blessing. And as long as I look at it from that perspective, every struggle that I have is worth it. You know, because God saw fit, because he knew that I could raise a child, I can handle the struggles. (personal communication, 2004)

The life values imparted through the African-centered education at the Faizah Shule appeared to have an impact on the participants in the study, which continued into their postsecondary lives. The young people spoke of moving into leadership roles when they attended institutions of higher learning. They also related how the principles of the Nguzo Saba were internalized and manifested in their daily choices and even in child rearing strategies. These life values also impacted the decision to have children, especially when these young women were not married. Yet, their beliefs in the sanctity of life and the blessings that children bring, which are African cultural traditions, coupled with their spirituality, anchored their resolve to adapt and reconcile an unexpected turn of events into their life's journey.

However, to imply that all of the experiences of the participants were in harmony with the Shule's philosophy and purpose would be misleading. In fact, many of the participants shared experiences that at some point were counter to the "positive" experiences of their peers.

8.   BLEMISHES IN THE TREASURE!

I'm like everyone else—I see the world in terms of what I would like to see happen, not what actually does. (Coelho & Clarke, 1988/1993, p. 29)

As the participants shared their experiences with me, I discovered there were some that did not find all aspects of them valuable. Some participants were quite colorful and candid in discussing their displeasure with specific components that shaped the education at the Shule. I was initially surprised by these exceptions, and much like Santiago, I had to acknowledge that perhaps I had viewed this experience in terms of what I would like to see happen. In this chapter, I share the particularities of this experience as the participants have shared them.

Self-Esteem Challenges

Acquiring a positive self-concept and African identity is central to the Shule and the African-centered educational experience. Veritably, the young people in the study asserted that the educational experience grounded them in their psychic space. Asma affirmed, "You always or at least almost always [are] able to maintain your identity regardless of the space" (personal communication,

2004). However, for one participant, Naimah, maintaining her African identity was challenging. The source of this interpersonal struggle did not come
from those external to the African American community (i.e., non-Africans)
but rather from those whom we would unabashedly refer to as "sisters."

Naimah considered herself to be firmly grounded in who she was as an
African person and was confident nothing could shake her concept of herself.
However, she found that when she decided to join a Greek sorority at the university she was attending, she was shaken to her very core. Even though her
mother had belonged to a sorority in college, Naimah indicated the following:

> I made a lot of assumptions about people who are in sororities…. That they're elit-
> ist…. I got involved in the Black Student Union and I had a very positive experience,
> not with just one individual from a sorority but the sorority as a whole kind of chipped
> in to help me in an event that was stressing me out…. And I mean, it was the morning
> of and they were there…early and they chipped right in and they were…just, I mean,
> really, really helpful and they seemed very genuine and in that moment, I decided to
> try to be a little more fair in my assessment. (personal communication, 2004)

Naimah felt that she was in a tug-of-war. On the one hand, she didn't want to
be associated with a negative organization, but as she researched Black soror-
ities, she discovered that they had a history of being influential and positive
within the African American community. She acknowledged this discovery:

> I started doing the research and understanding the history of the sororities and the sig-
> nificant contributions and just [the] strides that they had made for African American
> students in the university setting, which was never really explored at [the Faizah
> Shule] school. So it was this new history [and] it was beautiful and they struggled and
> they fought and that was right up my alley. So that sold me on the sorority because it
> was culturally and historically significant. (personal communication, 2004)

Naimah thought that the pledging process for the sorority would be much
like the rites-of-passage program at the Shule. She thought that there would
be sisterly bonding with challenging tasks to perform, but she never dreamed
that it would become such a demeaning experience. She felt that the sorority
set up divisiveness between the young African American women and encouraged competition between them on issues that had no substance, such as a
name or personality: "It's not healthy for a young person who is coming into
themselves, is learning who they are, and deciding who or what they want to
be" (personal communication, 2004). Since Naimah felt that she was well
grounded in her identity and self-concept, she chose to have the experience:

I also had the attitude that I was only going to accept certain things.... I wasn't going to allow myself to be hazed. I wasn't going to allow anybody to disrespect me. And...not only was I not going to allow it to happen to me but I wasn't going to allow it to happen to anybody else in my presence.... And I also felt like there are probably a lot of things that go on within the organization that are not legitimate but I can change it...and especially because I was going through it with my best friend and...we were just going to take it over...that was how I was thinking when I was 20.... And so the idea was to kind of infiltrate the organization...and turn it into this wonderful, powerful organization on campus. But what I found was that... it's difficult for anybody to sustain that type of consistent...demeaning and defiling of your person without saying anything back or without.... You're thinking that you're dealing with it...[but] it makes you question who you are...and yeah, all I can say is that it made me question the woman that I thought that I was. Like you know, if you're this dynamic Black woman, how did you end up here? (personal communication, 2005)

Naimah said she felt guilty for allowing herself to be in that situation. She confessed the following:

The biggest part that I had to go through, what I had to really heal from was being upset with me. It wasn't necessarily the women who I was angry at. It was me that I couldn't forgive.... Because I felt like...these other people, they don't have anything to lean back on. They don't have a point of reference. They don't know who you are. You do. And you allowed this to happen.... It broke me down...and that's the idea. You hear anybody talk about the process, they say [they] break you down, so that they can build you back up. They want to break everybody down so everybody is at zero together, and then we all come up and grow together. But I was broke down, I was broke down financially, emotionally, mentally, academically, spiritually, physically. I lost all my weight. I mean any way you can imagine; I was totally broken. (personal communication, 2005)

Naimah continued:

I was totally broke and that was the moment when I tried a lot things.... You know, I was ashamed so I couldn't really go to my family about it. And I couldn't really explain it to my friends because it's still hard for me to explain how I ended up in that situation. And so it got to the point where I was feeling so worthless that...I went to a psychologist at the school...they diagnosed me as clinically depressed.... But you know, nothing helped and I decided to go to church one day. They were having a youth chorale concert, a gospel concert. And I went and from then on...the Lord really changed my life. It really showed me what I went through and really gave me permission to forgive myself. (personal communication, 2005)

Drawing on her spiritual foundation, which she received both in her home environment and at the Shule, Naimah was able to make sense of her experience with the sorority. She offered this rationale as to how and why an African-centered person would join a fraternity or sorority:

> I think that I convinced myself that it was okay because of the historical significance that sorority had played. So that's how an African centered person could possibly conceive of joining a fraternity or sorority…another part of it is that…because my best friend who went to the Shule class with me and another brother who graduated with us at the school, he went [to a PWI], too. So I think another part of it is the fact that we were so isolated from our…mainstream [African centered] culture…when we got to college…we didn't want to be wild because, we still had good judgment skills. But we wanted to have fun. You know, we wanted to have a college experience. And we did not want to remain isolated. So I think that that part of the reason why we gravitated towards those organizations is because we wanted to belong and we wanted to have fun. (personal communication, 2005)

Rites-of-Passage Challenges

The rites-of-passage program was initiated into the African-centered educational experience as a means of assisting the transition of young people into adulthood. Most participants spoke of the experience affirmatively, but not all participants viewed the program positively. In fact, one participant, Adofo, provided an account of his discontent with the program.

He explained that he participated in the first rites, which was the adult rites-of-passage program, but he didn't participate in the Baba rites because he was away at college: "I didn't do the Baba rites [because] I was in Alabama. But you can't be labeled a Baba until you go through your adult rites [meaning adulthood]." When asked if he would go back and take his Baba rites, Adofo had prerequisites for taking that action. "I would [do it] depending on if certain people came back and did it…so if certain people came back, like the people who took me through my regular rites…I'll do it." (personal communication, 2005)

Adofo felt that many of the instrumental adult males (i.e., teachers and men of the community) had become distracted with other issues in their lives and were not available to oversee the rites-of-passage program for young men. He commented that he feels the rites-of-passage program "is not as potent" today as when those before him went through it. So he considered himself to be in rebellion:

I don't want to say I'm rebelling, but I don't want to go through it as it is right now because…you don't get anything from it…. I do rebel against [it] because I've done it once and I don't feel that you have to do that to be labeled a man. (personal communication, 2005)

In fact, contrary to the African cultural perspective of life transitions, Adofo offered the following: "You shouldn't have to go through this process every time you want to progress in life…. I've done it once and it's not easy…. It's demanding" (personal communication, 2005). He felt that his transition into manhood had been apparent by his life choices and the positive progression of his life.

Peer Perception Challenges

Many of the participants acknowledged that they were perceived as different by having attended an African-centered school. The educational experience provided them with a different lens to view events and the world. Asma shared that she felt there were very few people in the nation who could say that they had attended an African-centered school for most of their K–12 educational journey:

I tell people that children who are now adults like me…there may be about 20 of us and I don't mean here in the city, I mean period…. Maybe 25. I think that there are five that I have never seen. (personal communication, 2005)

Kamau considered the students in his cohort to have been the "experimental kids" because the school kept expanding its grades to accommodate the cohort. Another participant, Nina, spoke of being different, explaining how she felt like she was not "normal" as a result of the educational experience:

When you're in high school and middle school, you really just want to be like everybody else. You always want to be great. You know, [but] you just want to be normal. You want to be like the rest of the kids. You want to fit with the pack and roll with the punches. So while we're going through that teenage thing of not wanting to be great and wanting to be really normal, really regular, they [teachers] are pushing us to be great. (personal communication, 2004)

Nina noted that the knowledge acquired and the critical thinking skills engendered within her often made it difficult to communicate with peers in her neighborhood. She felt that her experience attending an African-centered school made her different and created a world that was "in a box," insulated from the "real world" and normalcy. Speaking of the community in which the Shule existed, Nina commented, "You know, the people outside in the community who were around us weren't really into that [an African-centered education]. So we had to deal with the dynamic of being in our little box" (personal communication, 2004). She continued:

> So we had to deal with going to the Shule and then going home and we had all these things we had learned, all these ideas we had developed, but those weren't the ideas of our peers that we were hanging out with after we got out of school. I mean as we grew older, we hung out with the people from the school.... But...when you go home, you sit on the porch and you talk to your friends from the neighborhood. These aren't the same things that they were learning in school. I mean, yes, we're learning African culture, but it went so much beyond that because...it wasn't what they were learning in school every day.... Every day you were confronted with the differences of the schools...and of the experience that we were having.... Even, sometimes it was on a small level, like we wore uniforms. But sometimes it was on ground levels like we had to do this science fair project every year and we had to apply the science fair project, how were they going to help African people. (personal communication, 2004)

While congregating with friends in her neighborhood, Nina noticed that she would sit back and listen to the conversations, often not commenting, but many times she challenged the thinking of her peers:

> They'd be talking about things or we'd be discussing things and I would...sit back and listen to them and I would say okay, well, that's not what I'm learning. What's the difference between what they're doing and what we're doing? Or what...it's kind of hard to explain because so...often you end up examining them as a person and the ideas that they're developing and the type of person they're developing into. And then you start looking at the experience that they had that's making them become this person...and I know hanging out with my friends sometimes, I would just have to stop, like I can't hang out with them right now...the people from the block because I always feel like I have such a broader view of things. I always am looking at things from so many angles and really examining and analyzing things as opposed to just taking it in. And just letting somebody tell me that's the way it is. (personal communication, 2004)

Athletics Challenges

Several participants mentioned the disadvantage of not having an athletics program at the Shule. Naimah's younger brother left the Shule in the 10th grade to pursue football at a traditional public school. In her brother's case,

Naimah's family had several uncles and cousins who had made it to the NBA in basketball, and family members were pressuring her mother and father to allow him to pursue his interest in sports. Adofo, who was a good friend of Naimah's brother, shared his understanding of Donald's choice to transfer from the FS/MGPA. Adofo explained the impact of not having an athletics program:

> A lot of people, like [Donald] for example, he left to go to Renaissance to play football because there was no football team [here]. We had a lot of good athletes come through there, too. There were some people who are making their name; going to college, right now. (personal communication, 2005)

Summary

Some of the participants related challenging incidents. For example, one participant expressed her difficulty in holding on to her African identity when she encountered a situation in an institution of higher learning. Although she does not bring indictment against the educational experience directly, she found that she was not able to stay grounded in her African womanness when she joined a sorority. Another participant spoke of his rebellion against the rites-of-passage program. He did not understand the value in participating in the second rites or the Baba rites and decided that he would not perform the second passage program. Another participant shared that the educational experience made her feel different than her peers, often to the point of not being able to communicate with them. Several participants shared how the lack of having an athletics program was an impetus for some young people to leave the Shule and seek athletic opportunities.

Through the collective efforts of African American families, the Faizah Shule was created and began instructing children from an African-centered educational model in 1974. The Shule expanded to the FS/MGPA, which was a K–12 institution, in 1992. As a CIBI member, the Shule collaborated with other African-centered institutions to develop guidelines, such as the CIBI position statement in 1994 for operating an African-centered institution. Integrating the position statement with its educational philosophy and purpose statement, the Shule provided an African-centered educational experience for African American students, specifically, the young people in this study.

From the analysis, I discovered four outcomes for this educational experience. The *first* outcome was that the Shule provided young people with an educational experience grounded in the concept of nation building. For the Shule, nation building is focused on the reclamation and restructuring of the African American communities and African reality. The participants in the study recounted their experiences in the Shule that fostered their understanding of nation building, which is supported and made successful through the family and community. The Shule positioned itself as family within the young people's lives. As articulated by the participants, the Shule was the extended family, and there was no doubt in their minds that the staff's interest in them was genuine.

The *second* outcome was that the Shule provided an educational experience for young people that cultivated their cultural knowledge and identity. The FS/MGPA believed that its students must know their cultural history and that "an African identity is embedded in the continuity of African cultural history" (CIBI, 2005, p. 7). The process of cultivating students' cultural knowledge and African identity was undertaken through acquiring cultural proficiency, cultivating positive self-concept, fostering greatness by the Shule community, and developing higher order thinking skills. The participants shared that they felt they were grounded in their African identity and appreciated the experience of examining phenomena from an African-centered perspective. The participants also were appreciative of the Shule community's declared belief in their "giftedness" and its unwavering resolve to foster their greatness.

The *third* outcome from the analysis was that the Shule provided an educational experience for young people that cultivated the principles of self-advocacy. At the Shule, self-advocacy in students was cultivated through social and political activism and student agency. Participants in this study recounted active involvement in political protest events. The young people also mentioned performing African drum and dance throughout the African American community as social activism. Student agency was encouraged when the Shule began to accept a new clientele after becoming a charter school. The young people agreed that they stepped into the roles of leadership to secure and maintain the integrity of the Shule environment.

The *fourth* outcome was that the Shule provided an educational experience for young people that developed their personhood. The staff at the Shule accepted responsibility as a community in the holistic education of their students and to assist students in evolving as responsible leaders within the African community. The means they were employed to advance the development of young people as adults through spirituality, rites of passage, and life values. The participants understood that spirituality was fundamental to the African ethos. They recalled the rites-of-passage program as a ritual and ceremony necessary for passage into adulthood. They shared how they acquired values from traditional African culture that they have integrated into their repertoire for decision making in their lives from the educational experience at the Shule.

Finally, from the data analysis it was revealed that some participants had challenging experiences. Even though many of the young people in the study espoused a positive educational experience at the FS/MGPA, there were accounts of discordance. For example, for one participant, although the educational experience grounded her in African cultural knowledge and developed within her a strong African identity, she encountered a challenge in higher education that made her reevaluate her identity. Another participant felt that the rites-of-passage program as required by the Shule was not a necessary ritual for adulthood transition and refused to participate in the second rites. Feeling different was noted by one participant as an uncomfortable consequence of receiving an African-centered education. She felt that the educational experience made it difficult for her to relate to her peers who had not attended an African-centered school. And several participants spoke of the lack of intramural sports or an athletics program as a disadvantage of attending the African-centered school.

In the next chapter, I present a discussion on the information shared by the participants. The tensions and challenges that the young people reported from the experience of attending an African-centered school are examined. Also examined is the question of whether an African-centered educational model or aspects of it can be implemented within a traditional public school setting. Finally, questions and suggestions for further research are presented.

9. BACK AT THE SYCAMORE TREE

"Every second of the search is an encounter with God," the boy told his heart. "When I have been truly searching for my treasure, every day has been luminous, because I've known that every hour was a part of the dream that I would find it. When I have been truly searching for my treasure, I've discovered things along the way that I never would have seen had I not had the courage to try things that seemed impossible for a shepherd to achieve." (Coelho & Clarke, 1988/1993, p. 90)

The purpose of this journey was to seek an understanding of the experiences of African American young people who attended an African-centered school. Further, I sought to discover and uncover nuances that made the young people's experiences unique to an African-centered education. The question that guided my search was this: "What are the educational experiences of African American young people who attended an African-centered school?"

In simplistic terms, the findings indicate that the young people experienced an education at the FS/MGPA that focused on four themes, but these themes had layers of complexity that were also addressed. These themes encompassed the following outcomes:

- The Shule provided experiences that advanced the concept of nation building.

- The Shule provided experiences that cultivated the cultural selves and African identity of the students.
- The Shule provided experiences that cultivated the principles of self-advocacy within the young people.
- The Shule provided experiences that developed the personhood of the young people.

The African-Centered Educational Experience

A review of the literature revealed that an African-centered educational model can be succinctly expressed as "the codification or systematic expression of African people's will to recover, recreate, and perpetuate [African] cultural heritage" (Akoto, 1994, pp. 320–321). In other words, an African-centered education provides an education to African American students that first centers the students within their own worldview systems (i.e., epistemology, ontology, axiology, and cosmology). This is accomplished by providing an experience that acknowledges and incorporates African culture and the African historical continuum into the educational experience. Participants shared experiences of learning from an African-centered frame of reference in which African people were subjects of history rather than objects, and the most poignant question for studying phenomena was, "how will this help African people?"

Fundamentally, the goal of this education "is to build commitment and competency within the present and future generations to support the struggle for liberation and nationhood of African people on the Continent and in the Diaspora" (CIBI, 2005, p. 6). The main goal of an African-centered education is to "reconnect, confirm and affirm students' cultural and communal identities and empower them to [transform] society through true education" (Shockley, 2003, p. 131). Shockley (2003) further explicated that one way this is achieved is through the concept of nation building and fostering communal environments. As aforementioned, the broad scope of this educational experience was to prepare young people for global participation, and simultaneously, to provide experiences in coursework commensurate with traditional public schools, such as mathematics, history, English, science, and others.

From the findings, the participants articulated experiences that overwhelmingly aligned with the espoused outcomes of the Shule. As to the extent of the depth of these outcomes that are intended for competency in students, this topic will have to be undertaken in another study. Within their narratives, the participants in this study reflected on learning about nation building and understanding the importance of the concept toward the liberation of African people from hegemonic oppression resulting from White supremacy. Drawing from the African traditional culture, family environment is essential to the community of the Shule and African-centered education. The young people discussed the importance of community and family in their educational experience and told how the Shule community became their extended family, with all of the benefits of a safe and stable environment.

In an African-centered education, teachers must have knowledge of African culture and also must be engaged in the perpetuation and liberation of African people. They must believe in the greatness of African people and employ African-centered pedagogy in the instruction of African American students. Findings revealed that participants in this study spoke of developing a positive self-concept from nurturing teachers who were willing to invest time, energy, and love in them and expected "greatness" from them. Higher ordered thinking skills were developed within students to ensure that this greatness was achieved.

In African traditional culture, spirituality encompasses all that is in life and also includes education, whether formal or informal. Spirituality is essential to individual progression through life, and the community is responsible for ensuring those life transitions through rituals and ceremonies. The participants perceived personhood to be vital to their experience at the Shule. They understood that spirituality was central to African cosmology, and they expressed comfort in acknowledging a power greater than themselves. The participants also cited the rites-of-passage program as a vehicle in which the Shule community assisted them in transitioning from childhood to adulthood. They also acknowledged that their feelings of commitment to the Shule community were fostered through the communal space that they had occupied while attending the Shule. Within this communal space, the participants discovered their roles to be pursued in the mission of nation building.

Much like the concept of *Sankofa,* the Shule reached back and fetched the African values system of Kemet, which was represented in the Maatian principles, and it also utilized the Nguzo Saba principles to impart traditional African values to its students. The young people in the study told how these values were integrated and utilized in the decision making aspects of their lives. These participants shared that they relied on these values as they interacted with their fellow peers while in the pursuit of higher education; they also shared that they passed these values and principles on to their children and utilized them in contemplating decisions of daily living.

Challenges and Tensions of the African-Centered Educational Experience

Yet there were challenges and tensions that resulted from the educational experience that were reported by the participants of the study but not found in the review of the literature. Overall, the participants spoke of the educational experience positively, but some expressed dissatisfaction with certain aspects of the experience. It appeared that this dissonance resulted from a lack of understanding of the values, principles, or even rituals surrounding activities in which the participants were expected to engage.

For instance, when Adofo spoke about the rites-of-passage program, he demonstrated a level of understanding of the purpose for participating in the rites program; however, having undergone the first rites-of-passage program, he refused to go through the second program. "I do rebel against [it] because I've done it once and I don't feel that you have to do that to be labeled a man" (personal communication, 2005). Underlying this rebellion is Adofo's frustration with what he perceived as the depreciation of the rites-of-passage program. He asserted that the program "is not as potent" (personal communication, 2005) and cited that the fathers and elders, who had been involved in providing the young men with the rites-of-passage experience, were now distracted with the issues of life, thus, in his view, the present rites-of-passage program does not provide a quality experience.

Did Adofo understand the importance of the rites-of-passage experience? Did he understand that in traditional African culture this experience is an essential ritual for making transitions through life? Did he understand that in some cultures, missing this experience would mean that a person was stuck in that stage until he or she made the passage? One could speculate that Adofo understood aspects of the rites-of-passage program, but he did not fully comprehend the importance of the rites for his development into personhood. The Shule community apparently "missed the mark" in maintaining its commitment and responsibility in assisting this young person through his life's transitions.

Another example that demonstrated tension with the educational experience was Nina's account of being different from her peers who attended traditional public schools. Some of the participants in the study enjoyed thinking of themselves as different from children who attended public schools. They considered their educational experiences as granting the opportunity to acquire superior intellectual skills and a broader perspective on the issues, locally, nationally, and globally. For Nina, being different was a double-edged sword because it permitted her to acquire knowledge and experience that many of her peers were not receiving in traditional public schools, yet it meant that she could not communicate readily with her neighborhood peers. She noted that she was constantly challenging the thinking of her friends on issues because she was encouraged and expected to analyze and deeply question events and observable facts. She found that her propensity for deep thinking often would have her sitting silently in the presence of her friends, and eventually, she just stopped hanging around them.

One study that speaks to Nina's dilemma was conducted by Amanda Datnow and Robert Cooper (1997). These authors examined how African American students attending predominantly White, elite, independent schools create formal and informal peer networks to support their academic success in these schools. Although the study examines the African American students' experience solely in a White, elite school, several findings have credence here. One finding indicated that the African American young people felt they were of a special group selected to attend these premier institutions and were expected to perform well academically. Another finding was that this educational experience often created a barrier of acceptance between them and their neighborhood peers. These students found that adopting the Eurocentric norms and values of the school made it easier for them to adapt to the school environment, but this cultural adoption occasioned stigma from their neighborhood peers.

In light of Datnow and Cooper's (1997) study, how does this "play out" for Nina? Attending the Shule meant that she had a different educational experience from her neighborhood peers. In an implicit way, it meant that she was "special" because she was engaged in an educational experience that the majority of her peers did not have the "privilege" of experiencing, since it was a tuition-based private school. Also, particular to Nina's educational experience was the adoption of the African-centered cultural traditions, manifested in disposition, values, dress, language, and other aspects. This cultural adoption was respected by the African American community and viewed in a positive context as cultural consciousness. However, the skills that Nina developed for interrogating and critically analyzing the world and her place in it became the "barbed wire fence" that separated her from her neighborhood peers. She often questioned the things that her peers took for granted, and she constantly sought to probe deeper for greater meaning in concepts that appeared to be obvious to her peers. Nina's educational experience provided and cultivated a broad base of knowledge on which she could draw that her neighborhood peers could not.

Another situation that was emblematic of the tensions and challenges that arose from this educational experience manifested when Naimah decided to join a sorority at the predominantly White institution she attended. Naimah's education at the Shule emphasized the values, principles, and traditions of African culture. Traditional African culture encourages the collectivity of African people and the importance of family and community. Values imparted through the Nguzo Saba provided Naimah with the foundation to take responsibility for her brothers and sisters (fellow students). She was encouraged to accept leadership positions in whatever environment she found herself, and she felt "grounded" in her African womanhood and identity and was able to maintain her space in any environment. Yet her educational experience at the Shule did not prepare her for encountering people of African descent whose lives were not guided by the values of traditional African culture.

Naimah was proficient in the historical heritage of the African and European encounters and had been given political insight for navigating a predominantly White institution, but she was naïve and unsuspecting when she found herself emotionally broken at the hands of her "sisters" in a Black sorority.

In his work, *African/Black Psychology in the American Context*, Kobi Kambon (1998) elucidated a disorder affecting the mental health of African American people, which he identified as "cultural misorientation." He posited that this disorder exists among African Americans as a consequence of Eurocentric oppression and African cultural suppression. The result of this disorder is the adoption of a Eurocentric worldview and Eurocentric self-consciousness by African Americans that manifest in anti-African behaviors and anti-African self-consciousness (Kambon, 1998).

Kambon's (1998) theory can be used to explain the behaviors of the sorority experience that strived to denigrate and "break" Naimah's self-confidence and identity on the premise that the community of sisters would rebuild her and others in the attempt to establish common ground and sisterhood bonding. On the surface, this act was reminiscent of the African rites-of-passage experience, where the spiritual, emotional, and physical well-being of the young girls were entrusted into the hands of capable, caring adults of the community. Much alike on the surface but under the illusion of a safe, caring, familial environment, for Naimah, the results of this experience raped her of her African grounding and left her "for dead" to find her own restoration.

In this educational experience, does the Shule have a responsibility to educate its young people on encountering African Americans who have adopted anti-African behaviors and provide strategies for negotiating these encounters? Should the values gained through the educational experience provide the fortitude and intuitive base to navigate these encounters? After a period of struggle, it seems that Naimah was able to draw strength through spirit to reground herself and regain focus.

How Is This Educational Experience Manifested?

In an examination of the lives of the young people and their location in life several years after graduating from the Shule, one could conclude that they left the educational experience with a repertoire of skills, insights, and values. Seemingly, at various decision points in their lives, they extracted skill sets acquired from the educational experience and employed them in ways that they perceived as most valuable for their lives. However, as discussed earlier, some of the young people had misunderstandings and challenges appropriating the skills and insights acquired through the educational experiences.

Were their lives a manifestation of the espoused goals of the educational experience? These young people were in pursuit of higher education, created families, and established careers. At first glance, these activities appear to be no different from the activities of students who graduated from traditional public schools. These endeavors are the pursuits of life. Yet what makes these undertakings different is that the fundamental ideological impetus for these activities is grounded in Black Nationalism and Pan-Africanism. The majority of the participants acknowledged the understanding that everything that they pursued was about nation building for African people on the continent and in the diaspora.

Essential to nation building is the establishment of institutions. Some ways in which these young people were obviously engaged in institution building were through volunteering at the Shule and other African American organizations as a means to ensure the Shule's continuance. They were also establishing institutions through families, because family is considered one of the central institutions in nation building. Also, Naimah and Heimis expressed plans for opening their own business.

These young people obtained higher education because they believed, as did their ancestors, that education would equip them with the tools to manage and maintain an independent nation of African people. As Naimah shared, "I feel like I was taught that education and everything that I do is about nation building. And if it's not about nation building, it is not about nothing" (personal communication, 2004).

The concept of Pan-Africanism was not apparent in the lives of these students. No one announced or demonstrated an overt economic or political link with African nations, such as an exchange of commerce or African political affiliations. However, several of the young people interviewed expressed an interest in creating links in their lives with Africans dispersed throughout the world. On a personal level, Naimah shared that she had dated a man who was Puerto Rican: "A lot of people feel like well, he's not black. Well, yes, he is… they [are] mixed with the Spanish and African people, so his complexion may be not as dark as mine, but he has a history of slavery just like I do" (personal communication, 2004). Another participant, Asma, not only dated but married a Bahamian. She acknowledged that the Bahamians have experienced the same historical struggles as Africans worldwide.

Concerns That Arose from the African-Centered Educational Experience

The Faizah Shule was created by a collective of African American middle-class families who were influenced by the Black Power movement during the late 1960s. As these parents were developing in Black Nationalist and Pan-Africanist thought and ideology, they realized the importance of agency and self-determinism. For these parents, an education immersed in African culture became a necessary component for the educational experience of their children.

Different Home Culture

Throughout much of the Shule's existence, it was an independent Black institution with an African-centered educational focus. It was a small, private school, and parents were required to pay tuition for their children to attend. Parents who sought to enroll their children in the schools were of two types: (a) parents who maintained African cultural practices within the home and wanted their children to have that experience in school, and (b) parents who were dissatisfied with the public schools and were looking for a "good" school for their children. The majority of the parents were of the former type of parent. Many of the parents who were of the latter type found that the parental involvement that was mandated as part of their child's enrollment facilitated personal transformation as they gained knowledge of African cultural traditions and identity.

When the Shule converted to an African-centered charter school, enrollment opened to all students within the FCSD. This open enrollment meant that the Shule began to experience a different clientele of students. Although the new clientele did consist of students whose parents were interested in immersing their children in African culture, the majority of those parents were just interested in their child attending a "good" school. Included in these two groups were parents who had neither interest nor time to be involved with the school. The Shule requested parental involvement through volunteerism at the school and attendance at training sessions on African culture, but it could not make it a condition of students' continual enrollment at the school. The student enrollment increased from approximately 60 students to nearly 250 students.

The Shule began to experience a mismatch of the school culture with the home culture. That is, when the home culture was aligned with the Shule's focus on traditional African culture and values or when the home culture reflected African American middle-class values, the school community and the home environment experienced cultural congruence. However, when the home culture aligned with the mainstream cultural values, that is, a White, middle-class focus, the Shule experienced a disconnect in forming a community between the home environment and the school environment. Also, when the home culture did not reflect mainstream values or African American middle-class values or even traditional African cultural values, it was evident to the Shule community that the home culture did not align with the school culture and hindered the formulation of community with those families. As previously espoused, community is fundamental to the African-centered educational experience.

There is much research in the literature that speaks to the incongruence between the home culture and the school culture regarding the traditional public schools and children of color, immigrants, and poor children (Irvine, 1990; Ladson-Billings, 1994). This issue is generally experienced in the traditional public school, because the culture of the school is reflective of mainstream culture that is established on White, middle-class values and worldviews, while the home culture of African Americans is established on African American values and worldviews. Some African American students' parents, particularly middle-class African Americans, have adopted the mainstream cultural values; consequently, these children are more likely to experience greater academic success in the public schools (Fordham, 1988; Irvine, 1990). However, for most African American students, their home culture does not align with the mainstream culture of the public school, which results in mis-understandings and low academic performance.

Surprisingly, after the conversion of the Shule from a private school to a charter school, cultural incongruence began to emerge as a pressing issue. This issue is dealt with lightly in this study, but it is a topic that deserves further research. The participants of the study alluded to the cultural incon-gruence when they recounted situations in which they accepted leadership and responsibility for maintaining the cultural integrity of their school. They spoke of students who had previously attended public schools and were now attending the Shule. These incoming students had no knowledge of African culture nor were they interested in learning about their African cultural her-itage. They were there simply because their parents were looking for a good school.

The philosophy of the Shule acknowledges that family involvement in student learning is essential to the formation of the community that is nec-essary for the academic and life success of the students. Mama Taraji men-tioned the difficulty that she and the Shule staff experienced in attempting to convince some parents that their involvement was critical to the success of their child(ren). It appeared that the lack of African cultural knowledge or the desire to acquire it for themselves and their children has created a major challenge for the Shule community to overcome to accomplish its goal of African cultural reclamation and nation building for the liberation of African people.

All That African Stuff

The participants appreciated the experience of the study of phenomenon from a position centered in their African cultural heritage. They spoke of learning about world civilization, originating in Kemet rather than Greece. They learned about the institution of slavery from the perspective of the kid-napped Africans. They studied the African classics, investigated solutions to problems affecting African people, celebrated the lives of African and African American ancestors, were able to openly acknowledge their spirituality, stud-ied African nations, and operated in and honored the worldview systems of African people.

Some students and parents perceived the immersion into the African cul-tural heritage and epistemology at the Shule as overbearing. The question arose, "Why do we have to learn all this African stuff?" One parent stated that she was concerned that her children (three attended the Shule) would be ill-equipped in college because they were not exposed to the classics of mainstream education:

> Some of those questions they have on tests that you take anywhere in society, they are all based on their white culture. So my kids weren't able to address that. At one time I felt kind of bad about it because I felt they [her children] weren't well rounded. (Mama Mariama, personal communication, 2004)

In fact, one of the participants acknowledged she felt somewhat handicapped when she took a history course in college and was not familiar with some of the information on European history. Should the African-centered educational experience guarantee that students are exposed to mainstream canons to ensure their academic success in higher education? Can an African-centered education maintain its cultural integrity and focus while teaching mainstream canons?

As a pluralistic society, America's borders are crossed every day by people from other nations for various reasons. The pursuit of higher education is one attraction that precipitates this influx of people. For most, instruction in the mainstream canons are not a prerequisite for the successful completion of their degree. Fully grounded in the educational canons from their home country, many international students successfully complete instruction in the Eurocentric institutions of America without loss of identity or cultural traditions.

Likewise, for African American students who attend African-centered schools. The cultural imperative of an African-centered education does not impede the academic success of the students whose education was delivered from an African worldview. In fact, a majority of the young people interviewed attended major universities; a large percentage of them attended PWIs and successfully completed their degrees. They attributed their ability to navigate the mainstream educational system to their cultural foundation cultivated and established in an African-centered education.

Can These Educational Benefits Be Attained in Public Schools?

Can the participants of this study receive these educational benefits from America's public schools?

Maybe

The answer to that question is that certainly there are aspects of this educational experience operating in some classrooms (e.g., effective teachers, African American curricula, small family environments, etc.). However, one hindrance to this educational experience is a refusal to recognize the impact of culture on the education of children, particularly African American children. Ladson-Billings (1994), along with other researchers, recognized that the American educational public school system refuses to acknowledge African Americans as a distinct cultural group (Irvine, 1990; Lee, 1992). She went on to say, "it is assumed that African American children are exactly like white children but just need a little extra help" (p. 9).

Certainly we know that African culture is not monolithic, since there are well over a thousand distinct groups of people on the continent and in the diaspora. However, research has revealed that there are many similarities among these cultures, such as cosmology, family and community relationships, and the importance of rituals, ceremonies, and traditions among the people (Mbiti, 1970; Tedla, 1995). Review of the literature indicates that culture is an essential piece to existence and gives meaning to reality for people. To ignore the culture of a people is to create barriers to understanding their needs and concerns and in effect to sabotage and hinder any effective communications. Lack of attention to the culture of African American children has perpetuated their academic difficulties in American schools.

Teacher and student interaction in public schools is where this disconnect of culture is most notable, since these students receive instruction from a predominantly White, middle-class, female teaching staff. It is plausible that this teaching staff has had minimum (if any) training on how to teach students of diverse cultures. Teachers' belief systems are shaped by the racially hegemonic influences on knowledge that emanate from within the dominant culture. So oftentimes, teachers hold beliefs about racial groups and cultures that are influenced by America's racist notions of designated "others."

Yet in some classrooms within public schools across the nation, students are experiencing a culturally relevant education. This experience is the result of teachers not limited to the African American race, who are described by Ladson-Billings (1994) as effective in creating academic success with African American children. These teachers are advocates for social justice and parental and community involvement in the educational process of students and hold high expectations for all students and their abilities to learn. But these pockets of effective instruction to African American children are the exception rather than the norm.

The majority of African American students in public schools are not having these experiences. Education for them is a process of marginalization, de-Africanization, and de-humanization. African American students graduate from public schools without the knowledge of their cultural origins, historical contributions to civilization, the African Holocaust (Maafa), and contributions to American society as well as the global society. Neither have they been given the political capital for navigating mainstream society.

Maybe Not

Education in society serves a functional purpose by providing the conduit through which the national culture is maintained and perpetuated. According to Akoto (1992), education "...lies at the very core of the nation, as it involves the codification, perpetuation, interpretation and transmission of the national history and culture..." (p. 41). Based on the aforementioned purpose of education, one should expect that the objectives of the American public school are to promote the perpetuation of American culture and society.

Within the literature, researchers have asserted that African American children are culturally different from European American children. In fact, research supports the premise that African people and European people operate from different worldview systems that are fundamental to how these groups make sense of the world or their construction of reality (Akoto, 1992; Ani, 1994; Hilliard, 1997; Kambon, 1998). Kambon (1998), in his work, *African/Black Psychology in the American Context*, clearly delineated these worldview systems into four categories: (a) cosmological, (b) ontological, (c) axiological, and (d) epistemological.

Kambon (1998) posited that an African cosmological perspective is based on interdependence, collectivism, and the oneness of human nature, whereas the European cosmology is established on separateness, independence, and the conflict of human nature. He proposed that the African ontological perspective is that all things are spiritual and interrelated, whereas the Europeans believe that the essential nature of reality is material. Kambon further theorized that the African axiology places emphasis on interpersonal interactions and relationships, while the European basic value system focuses on person-to-object relationships. Finally, he stated that Africans utilize an affective-cognitive synthesis as a way of knowing reality, while the European epistemology is based on cognitive over affective processes in knowing reality.

Based on Kambon's (1998) research, implementing an African-centered educational model similar to the one presented in this study would be at odds with the existing worldview systems of the American public schools. The American public schools were initially created and have been maintained through the European worldview system. This system mirrors the national worldview and fulfills the purpose of the perpetuation of American society.

In light of the fact that schools are machines employed in the continuance of American society, it is safe to conclude that some aspects of an African-centered educational experience cannot be found in traditional public schools. These components of the African-centered educational model that reside in the concept of African nation building, spirituality, and the impartation of life values, may be in conflict with the dominant cultures' societal goals. It does not serve the self-interest of the elite of American society to promote the nation building interest of African American people. Seemingly, it would be a case of insanity for Americans to teach the concepts of nation building for the development and liberation of another nation within itself. Particularly, it would be insanity to provide this instruction to a people that they have historically held in low regard and as an inferior people. Would not this action be equivalent to the nation of Israel educating the Palestinian people in the concepts of nation building? How could the outcome possibly benefit its national objectives?

I conclude that the concept of African nation building cannot be taught in American public schools. It does not serve the interests of American society to educate African American children for their liberation and advancement (Carnoy, 1974; Freire, 1976; Shujaa, 1994). Instructions in spirituality and imparting life values that are fundamental to an African-centered education are taboo within the American public school system. Consequently, introducing an African-centered educational model into the public schools would be like introducing a foreign agent into the bloodstream. This action would disturb the equilibrium of the environment and the white blood cells would attempt to adapt the foreign agent to the environment or destroy it. They could not coexist.

Recommendations

Fundamental to the African-centered educational model presented in this study are the concepts of African nation building, spirituality, African cultural traditions, and African values. These concepts proceed from the African worldview systems that center Africans within their own epistemology, ontology, cosmology, and axiology. This centeredness, according to Asante (1988/2003), places African people as agents of their history rather than objects of it. This educational model must

1. Proceed from the ideology of nation building.
2. Be undergirded by African cultural history and identity.
3. Be permeated by the spirituality of African people through traditions, rituals, and ceremonies.
4. Be taught by people who themselves are engaged in re-Africanization and who are actively promoting the advancement of African people.
5. Be African centered in both curriculum and pedagogy.

In contrast, the traditional public school model is a nationalist model that promotes the concept of White or European nation building for American and other European nations and its allies, particularly those that align with the ideology of the primacy of Western culture. In public schools, federal legislation has prescribed the separation of church and state, interpreted to mean that schools do not endorse religious practices within the school environment (Cline, 2006). Specifically, the law states that the government cannot endorse a particular religious dogma and mandate students to practice it, but religion is not synonymous with spirituality in the African perspective. Additionally, there have been ongoing debates within the educational community over who should be responsible for imparting values to students in schools (Gibbs, 2006), asking the following: "Should character education or values be imparted solely through the home environment or should the school be an integral player in passing values on to children?

The aforementioned educational ideology for traditional public schools reflects the Eurocentric worldview system of American society, which guides the curriculum and the pedagogy in the educational institutions and would present challenges and impediments to the implementation of an African-centered education model. In the classroom, the primary source of instruction is the teacher. Research has revealed that teachers' beliefs about the students they teach has an impact on student success or failure (Irvine, 1990; Ladson-Billings, 1994). As members of society, teachers' beliefs are shaped and influenced through the socialization of American society. The historical legacy of racism and European hegemony of American society in its relationship to African Americans is manifested in teachers' beliefs and expectations.

The challenge for American schools interested in implementing an African-centered educational model would be to attempt instruction of this model with teachers who do not believe in the academic and intellectual capabilities or the cultural relevancy of African American children. According to proponents of an African-centered educational model, it must be instructed by teachers who believe in their students' abilities, who respect and are knowledgeable of African culture and are actively working toward the liberation of African people.

An aspect of this educational model may be implemented successfully in the traditional public school setting. This study revealed that teachers in the African-centered educational model were effective instructors of African American students. These teachers demonstrated personal traits and attitudes that led to their students' academic success, similar to the research conducted by Ladson-Billings (1994). These effective teachers (a) believe that all children can succeed, (b) create a personal connection to students and their communities, (c) assist students in developing and understanding their cultural identity, (d) use students' culture to facilitate learning, and (e) promote and encourage critical and creative ways of knowing. Demonstrating these attitudes and traits, teachers were able to energize and motivate African American students to achieve academic success. This study affirms Ladson-Billings's research and provides empirical evidence to substantiate the importance of teachers' attitudes, beliefs, and expectations in impacting African American student achievement.

There are challenges and tensions for African-centered public academies in implementing this educational model that need consideration by policymakers. The Shule became a public academy during the attendance of the participants in my study. During the interviews, the young people, parents, and the director mentioned the struggles of this African-centered charter school as it attempted to fulfill its mission to provide an African-centered education while meeting the mandate for achievement on the state standardized tests. If policymakers are truly interested in creating a culturally relevant environment for African American students by implementing an African-centered educational model, they must create and incorporate avenues for the administrators and teachers of these schools to maintain the cultural focus while helping students to successfully achieve on standardized tests. This may mean that policy is created that allows these schools to be exempted from the mandated testing for a prescribed period of time to allow for the complete implementation of the educational model.

The intent of this study was not to conclude whether this educational experience for African American young people was better than a different educational experience (i.e., traditional public schools or private schools). Rather, the purpose of this research was to gain insight on how these young people perceive this educational experience and whether that experience aligned with the educational outcomes of the Shule.

Future Research

The participants highlighted the following experiences at the Shule: (a) the family and community environment, (b) the pursuit of African nation building, (c) spirituality, (d) the understanding of the African cultural heritage and history, (e) the acquisition of a positive self-concept, (f) the interaction with invested and concerned teachers, (g) the development of critical and creative thinking skills, and (h) the attainment of agency as well as activism. They also exposed some challenges and tensions with the educational experience. They affirmed that without this experience, they would not be the people that they are today.

The findings of this study create a multitude of unanswered questions that need to be further explored. What are the experiences of current students who attend the Shule in which the majority of their school experience has been as a charter school? The participants, parents, and school director in this study alluded to a cultural change in the environment with the influx of new students. Future research should investigate how current students perceive their educational experiences at the Shule.

Another question needs to be explored: "When students' educational experiences of attending an African-centered school are compared across different contexts, are those experiences similar?" Further research should compare the experiences of the young people in this study with those reported by students in another African-centered school. The comparison could examine students' experiences in an African-centered charter academy, an African-centered IBI, or an African-centered immersion public school.

How do African American young people who have graduated from a traditional public school perceive their educational experience and its impact on their lives? This question can be explored by a study that examines the educational outcomes of this African-centered educational model for African American students with the outcomes of African American students who attended a traditional public school.

For the purposes of assisting leadership in schools that primarily educate African American students, research should be undertaken that examines the leadership attitudes, values, and strategies of people who commit their lives to the education of this underserved population of students.

The insights garnered from further research in African-centered education can assist policymakers, educators, and parents in developing effective education of African American children. In efforts to fulfill the American vision of a pluralistic democratic nation in which all groups of people are benefactors of the U.S. Declaration of Independence, guaranteeing the right to "life, liberty, and the pursuit of happiness," further research on this educational model could provide the foundation on which to build equitable and liberatory education. The virtues of democracy and movement into globalization demand that America cannot continue to ignore and marginalize the gifts and talents of its entire people.

EPILOGUE

What you still need to know is this: before a dream is realized, the Soul of the World tests everything that was learned along the way. It does this not because it is evil, but so that we can, in addition to realizing our dreams, master the lessons we've learned as we've moved toward that dream. That's the point at which most people give up. It's the point at which, as we say in the language of the desert, one "dies of thirst just when the palm trees have appeared on the horizon." (Coelho & Clarke, 1988/1993, pp. 91–92)

Much like Santiago, it was a dream that started me on this journey. The universe was giving me an omen, speaking to me concerning my preparedness to create an optimal educational experience for children of color, specifically African American children. In my dream, I was leading the children toward a destination. The children were depending on me to safely lead them and moved in lockstep with me. They obediently followed my direction and only became distracted when I began to demonstrate my own ramping levels of unsoundness and concern. At that point, chaos and confusion prevailed and the conclusion of this virtuous and benign endeavor was destruction of the children while I looked on in paralyzed horror. I think what I found most challenging about the dream was that once the children began to seek their own solutions for the problem of crossing the street safely, I was unable to prevent the sad outcome.

So what is it that the universe is saying to me? I think that it was a warning—a warning of advisement to look deeper into the perceived problem. In the dream, a knowledge of the route that we were traveling, as well as traffic patterns and conditions, would have given me more insight into how to best navigate the path toward our destination. I could have chosen a different route, or selected a different time of travel, or divided the children into smaller groups, or even solicited more people to assist with supervision.

How does this apply to African-centered schools? I was interested in creating a school that would provide African American children with an education that would be a holistic model that would speak specifically to their worldview as descendants of Africa. At the time of the dream, I did not realize that I was standing on the shoulders of many African Americans who came before me and were asking the same question: "What is the optimal educational experience for African American children?" I also was not fully aware of the necessity of utilizing both an African-centered curriculum, as well as an African-centered pedagogy. Having one without the other would not ensure that the students were receiving an effective African-centered educational experience. I also discovered that there were specific tenets or protocols for defining an African-centered educational model. These tenets were derived by the CIBI and endorsed by Afrocentrists. This model could not be apportioned into benign versions to be acceptable to the traditional public school model; to be effective, it must exist as an entity unto itself. Acquiring this information provided the foundation of inquiry, as I explored the perspectives of former students as they shared their experiences with this educational model and their reflections of how the experience impacted their lives.

The lessons learned equipped me with a deeper and broader understanding of the desired educational outcomes for students of African descent. I appreciated the importance of nation building for African American students. It is necessary to understand that nation building was seen as occurring in the promotion of family and community. Yet as one participant pointed out, it can also happen in very obscure ways, such as giving someone a ride from the airport. I gained an awareness of the value of believing in the greatness of these human beings who enter into our classrooms. In my own experience of re-Africanization as I became intimate with the Shule, I also recognized the importance of rituals in African culture and the significance it plays in honoring the transitions in life. Yet most importantly profound for me was that I now understood the significance of spirituality within the educational process.

The African-centered educational model does not apologize for bringing spirituality into the educational experience. Traditional African culture recognizes that Spirit is in all things and that all matter is one; the King of Salem informed Santiago that all is just one (Coelho & Clarke, 1988/1993). Spirituality is not promoted as a religion; it is just an acknowledgment that there is some power bigger than us and we are intricately connected to all things and everyone. I believe that the spirituality component is the glue that ties all of the pieces together for this experience. It was reacquainting the participants to the cosmology of African people that enabled them to express their relationship to the world, their communities, their families, and to themselves. The participants shared that they knew they were responsible to the planet, to the animals, and to other human beings. As I understand it now, spirituality is the force that guides all beings through their journeys of this life. That is why I chose to refer to the book, *The Alchemist* (Coelho & Clarke, 1988/1993), as a guide for my story, this book, and this journey.

It was this spirituality that guided my steps through signs and omens in much the same way as Santiago was guided:

> *The boy knew what he was about to describe, though: the mysterious chain that links one thing to another, the same chain that had caused him to become a shepherd, that had caused his recurring dream, that had brought him to a city near Africa, to find a king, and to be robbed in order to meet a crystal merchant, and…. (Coelho & Clarke, 1988/1993, p. 49)*

My life experiences were linked to my dream and to dreams that placed me on the journey to discover and understand in greater depth the outcomes of an African-centered educational model. This journey brought me to locate an informant who led me to the school and the participants of this research. Finally, as a result of this exploration, I now can clearly acknowledge African-centered education as a model of education that can assist African American students in cultural reclamation. It is through this cultural reclamation steeped in the African cosmology of spirituality that students are able to hold their space in the world, become world changers, and promote Pan-Africanism, foundational to honoring the rights of all human beings. Most importantly to me, it is through spirituality that students can become intrinsic participants in the world around them.

Like Santiago, I always had the treasure with me. For me, it was the spirit‑
uality that set me on this course and the spirituality that would allow me to
hear the Soul of the World more clearly, and that is the language of love.
Santiago learned the language of the Soul of the World in the desert amidst
the silence, and I had the unique pleasure of learning this language through
the voices of these young people. These voices often remain in the silence and
are not heard, but for me, they sounded like thunder shouting to my ears and
hopefully to yours.

NOTES

Foreword

1. For a more detailed discussion of CIBI, see Lomotey (in press).
2. Piert elaborates on the Nguzo Saba in Chapter 3 of this volume.
3. Piert does an excellent job of expanding on this definition of African-centered education in Chapter 5.
4. Faizah Shule/Marcus Garvey Preparatory Academy (FS/MGPA) is a pseudonym.
5. In the final analysis, Piert's research question became this: What were the experiences of African American young people who attended an African-centered school?

Chapter 4

1. To ensure anonymity of the location and the participants for the purposes of this book, the names of the school, city, and people have been changed. The name of the school is significant to its philosophy. I used the term *Faizah* as the name of the school to mean life; however, Faizah is actually a Kiswahili term, which means "she is victorious." The participants referred to the Faizah Shule/Marcus Garvey Preparatory Academy, consisting of the elementary, middle, and high schools, as the *Shule*, which is a Kiswahili term for *school*. Henceforth, Faizah Shule/Marcus Garvey Preparatory Academy will be referred to as the acronym FS/MGPA, or simply as the Shule.

REFERENCES

Activism [British Dictionary Definition]. (n.d.). *Dictionary Online*. Retrieved from http://dictionary.reference.com/browse/activism?s=t

Agbo, A. H. (1999). *Values of Adinkra symbols*. Kumasi, Ghana: Ebony Designs and Publications.

Aisha Shule/W. E. B. DuBois Preparatory Academy. (1999). *Parent handbook*. Detroit, MI: Author.

Aisha Shule/W. E. B. DuBois Preparatory Academy. (2005). *Annual education report*. Detroit, MI: Author.

Akoto, A. (1992). *Nationbuilding: Theory and practice in Afrikan centered education*. Washington, DC: Pan Afrikan World Institute.

Akoto, A. (1994). Notes on an Afrikan-centered pedagogy. In M. J. Shujaa (Ed.), *Too much schooling, too little education: A paradox of Black life in White societies* (pp. 319–337). Trenton, NJ: Africa World Press.

Akoto, K. A., & Akoto, A. N. (2000). *The Sankofa movement: ReAfrikanization and the reality of war*. Washington, DC: Oyoko InfoCom.

Ani, M. (1980). *Let the circle be unbroken*. New York, NY: Nkonimfo Publications.

Ani, M. (1994). *Yurugu: An African-centered critique of European cultural thought and behavior*. Trenton, NJ: Africa World Press.

Anwisye, S. (1993). Education is more than the three "R"s. *Harvard Journal of African American Public Policy, 2*, 97–101.

Ansalone, G. (2009). *Exploring unequal achievement in the schools: The social construction of failure*. Lanham, MD: Lexington Books.

Asante, M. K. (2003). *Afrocentricity: The theory of social change*. Trenton, NJ: Africa World Press. (Original work published 1988)

Asante, M. K. (1991). The Afrocentric idea in education. *Journal of Negro Education, 60*(2), 170–180.

Asante, M. K. (2000). *The Asante principles for the Afrocentric curriculum*. Retrieved from http://www.asante.net/articles/6/the-asante-principles-for-the-afrocentric-curriculum/

Ballantine, J. H., & Hammack, F. M. (2011). *The sociology of education: A systematic analysis*. Upper Saddle River, NJ: Pearson Education.

Banks, J. A. (1998). The lives and values of researchers: Implications for educating citizens in a multicultural society. *Educational Researcher, 27*(7), 4–17.

Boykins, A. W. (1986). The triple quandary and the schooling of Afro-American children. In U. Neisser (Ed.), *The school achievement of minority children: New perspectives* (pp. 57–91). Hillsdale: L. Erlbaum Associates.

Brady, J. E., & Prufer, K. M. (1999). Caves and crystalmancy: Evidence for the use of crystals in ancient Maya religion. *Journal of Anthropological Research, 55*(1), 129–144.

Carnoy, M. (1974). *Education as cultural imperialism*. London, UK: Longman.

Clarke, J. H. (1991). *African world revolution: Africans at the crossroads*. Trenton, NJ: Africa World Press.

Clarke, J. H. (1994). The American antecedents of Marcus Garvey. In R. Lewis & M. Warner-Lewis (Eds.), *Garvey: Africa, Europe, the Americas* (pp. 1–16). Trenton, NJ: Africa World Press.

Cline, A. (2006). School prayers and Bible reading: Myths about the separation of church and state. *About Religion and Spirituality*. Retrieved from http://atheism.about.com/od/church-statemyths/a/PrayerBibleReadingCommon.htm

Coelho, P., & Clarke, A. R. (1993). *The alchemist*. New York, NY: HarperCollins. (Original work published 1988)

Council of Independent Black Institutions (CIBI). (2005) *About the Council of Independent Black Institutions*. Retrieved from http://www.cibi.org/newsite/index.html#/about-us

Darling-Hammond, L. (2014). Closing the achievement gap: A systemic view. In J. V. Clark (Ed.), *Closing the achievement gap from an international perspective* (pp. 7–20). Rotterdam, Netherlands: Springer.

Datnow, A., & Cooper, R. (1997). Peer networks of African American students in independent schools: Affirming academic success and racial identity. *Journal of Negro Education, 66*(1), 56–72.

Doughty, J. J. (1973). *A historical analysis of Black education* (Unpublished doctoral dissertation). The Ohio State University, Columbus.

Dream [Def. 1 & 2]. (n.d.). *Merriam-Webster Online*. Retrieved from http://www.merriam-webster.com/dictionary/dream

Ennis, R. H. (1987). A taxonomy of critical thinking dispositions and abilities. In J. B. Baron & R. J. Sternberg (Eds.), *Teaching thinking skills: Theory and practice* (pp. 9–26). New York, NY: W. H. Freeman.

Essien-Udom, E. U. (1962). *Black nationalism: A search for identity in America*. Chicago, IL: The University of Chicago Press.

Fordham, S. (1988). Racelessness as a factor in Black students' school success: Pragmatic strategy or pyrrhic victory? *Harvard Business Review, 58*(1), 54–84.

Freire, P. (1976). *Pedagogy of the oppressed.* New York, NY: Continuum.

Geertsen, H. R. (2003). Rethinking thinking about higher-level thinking. *Teaching Sociology, 31,* 1–19.

Gibbs, J. (2006). Internalizing character education values by living and learning within a caring school community. *TRIBES: A New Way of Learning and Being Together.* Retrieved from http://www.tribes.com

Giddings, G. J. (2001). Infusion of Afrocentric content into the school curriculum: Toward an effective movement. *Journal of Black Studies, 31*(4), 462–482.

Ginwright, S. A. (1999). *Identity for sale: The Afrocentric movement and the Black urban struggle in Oakland Public Schools* (Unpublished doctoral dissertation). University of California-Berkeley, San Diego.

Ginwright, S. A. (2004). *Black in school: Afrocentric reform, urban youth, and the promise of hip-hop culture.* New York, NY: Teachers College Press.

Glesne, C. (1999). *Becoming qualitative researchers: An introduction* (2nd ed.). Reading, MA: Addison Wesley Longman.

Hale, J. E. (1986). *Black children: Their roots, culture, and learning styles* (rev. ed.). Baltimore, MD: The Johns Hopkins University Press.

Hatch, J. A., & Wisniewski, R. (1995). *Life history and narrative.* London, UK: RoutledgeFalmer.

Hilliard, A. G., III. (1997). *SBA: The reawakening of the African mind.* Gainesville, FL: Makare Publishing.

hooks, b. (1993). *Sisters of the yam: Black women and self-recovery.* Toronto, Canada: Between the Lines.

Hotep, U. (2001). *Dedicated to excellence: An Afrocentric oral history of the Council of Independent Black Institutions, 1970–2000* (Unpublished doctoral dissertation). Duquesne University, Pittsburgh.

Irvine, J. J. (1990). *Black students and school failure: Policies, practices, and prescriptions.* New York, NY: Greenwood Press.

Kambon, K. K. (1998). *African/Black psychology in the American context: An African-centered approach.* Tallahassee, FL: Nubian Nation Publications.

Karenga, M. (1980). *Kawaida theory: An introductory outline.* Inglewood, CA: Kawaida.

Karenga, M. (1988). *Introduction to Black studies.* Los Angeles, CA: University of Sankore Press.

Karenga, M. (1989). *The African American holiday of Kwanzaa: A celebration of family, community and culture.* Los Angeles, CA: University of Sankore Press.

Kenyatta, K. (1998). *Guide to implementing Afrikan-centered education.* Detroit, MI: Afrikan Way Investments.

Konadu, K. (2005). *Truth crushed to the Earth will rise again: The East Organization and the principles and practice of Black nationalist development.* Trenton, NJ: Africa World Press.

Ladson-Billings, G. (1994). *The dreamkeepers: Successful teachers of African American children.* San Francisco, CA: Jossey-Bass.

Lee, C. D. (1992). Profile of an independent Black institution: African-centered education at work. *Journal of Negro Education, 61*(2), 160–177.

Lee, C. D. (1994). African-centered pedagogy: Complexities and possibilities. In M. J. Shujaa (Ed.), *Too much schooling, too little education: A paradox of Black life in White societies* (pp. 295–318). Trenton, NJ: Africa World Press.

Lomotey, K. (1992). Independent Black institutions: African-centered models. *Journal of Negro Education, 61*(4), 455–462.

Lomotey, K. (in press.) The Council of Independent Black Institutions. In M. J. Shujaa & K. Shujaa (Eds.), *The encyclopedia of African cultural heritage in North America.* Thousand Oaks, CA: Sage.

Maglangbayan, S. (1972). *Garvey, Lumumba, and Malcolm: Black national-separatists.* Chicago, IL: Third World Press.

Mbiti, J. S. (1970). *African religions and philosophy.* Garden City, NY: Anchor Books.

Menkiti, I. A. (1984). Person and community in African traditional thought. In R. A. Wright (Ed.), *African philosophy: An introduction* (pp. 171–181). Lanham, MD: University Press of America.

Miles, M. B., & Huberman, A. M. (1994). *Qualitative data analysis: An expanded sourcebook.* Thousand Oaks, CA: Sage.

Moses, W. J. (1978). *The golden age of Black nationalism 1850–1925.* Hamden, CT: Archon Books.

Mungazi, D. A. (1996). *Gathering under the mango tree: Values in traditional culture in Africa.* New York, NY: Peter Lang.

Murrell, P. C., Jr. (1999). Chartering the village: The making of an African-centered charter school. *Urban Education, 33*(5), 565–583.

Murrell, P. C., Jr. (2002). *African-centered pedagogy: Developing schools of achievement for African American children.* Albany: The State University of New York Press.

Nobles, W. W. (1990). The infusion of African and African American content: A question of content and intent. In A. G. Hilliard III, L. Payton-Stewart, & L. O. Williams (Eds.), *Infusion of African and African American content in the school curriculum* (pp. 5–26). Chicago, IL: Third World Press.

Ochs, E., & Capps, L. (1996). Narrating the self. *Annual Review of Anthropology, 25*, 19–43.

Okafor, V. O. (1996). The place of Africalogy in the university curriculum. *Journal of Black Studies, 26*(6), 688–712.

Orfield, G., Eaton, S. E., & Harvard Project on School Desegregation. (1996). *Dismantling desegregation: The quiet reversal of Brown v. Board of Education.* New York, NY: New Press.

Permutt, P. (2009). *The complete guide to crystal chakra healing: Energy medicine for mind, body, and spirit.* New York, NY: Cico Books.

Pollard, D. S., & Ajirotutu, C. S. (2000). *African-centered schooling in theory and practice.* Westport, CT: Bergin & Garvey.

Rashid, H. M., & Muhammad, Z. (1992). The Sister Clara Muhammad schools: Pioneers in the development of Islamic education in America. *The Journal of Negro Education, 61*(2), 178–185.

Ratteray, J. D., & Shujaa, M. J. (1987). *Dare to choose: Parental choice at independent neighborhood schools*. Washington, DC: U.S. Department of Education.

Ravitch, D. (1990). Multiculturalism: E pluribus plures. *American Scholar, 59*(3), 337–354.

Redkey, E. S. (1969). *Black exodus: Black nationalist and back-to-Africa movements, 1890–1910*. New Haven, CT: Yale University Press.

Richards, D. M. (1989). *Let the circle be unbroken: African spirituality in the diaspora*. Trenton, NJ: The Red Sea Press. (Original work published 1980)

Robinson, C. L. (2004). *Reconceptualizing the implications of Eurocentric discourse vis-a-vis the educational realities of African American students with some implications for special education* (Unpublished doctoral dissertation). Miami University, Oxford, Ohio.

Rockquemore, K. (1997). Afrocentric education. In C. Herring (Ed.), *African Americans and the public agenda: The paradoxes of public policy* (pp. 190–206). Thousand Oaks, CA: Sage.

Salaam, A. (2013). *Is the White man still the devil: The nation of Islam, (the honorable) Elijah Muhammad and Malcolm X*. Victoria, BC, Canada: Friesen Press.

Schlesinger, A. M., Jr. (1992). *The disuniting of America*. New York, NY: W. W. Norton.

Shade, B. J. (1994). Understanding the African American learner. In E. R. Hollins, J. E. King, & W. C. Hayman (Eds.), *Teaching diverse populations: Formulating a knowledge base* (pp. 175–189). Albany: The State University of New York Press.

Shaull, R. (2003). Foreword. In P. Freire (Ed.), *Pedogogy of the oppressed* (pp. 29–34). New York, NY: Continuum Press. (Original work published in 1970)

Shockley, K. G. (2003). *When culture and education meet: An ethnographic investigation of an Africentric private school in Washington D.C.* (Unpublished doctoral dissertation). University of Maryland, College Park.

Shujaa, M. J. (1992). Afrocentric transformation and parental choice in African American independent schools. *The Journal of Negro Education, 61*(2), 148–159.

Shujaa, M. J. (1994). *Too much schooling, too little education*. Trenton, NJ: Africa World Press.

Somé, S. (1999). *Welcoming spirit home: Ancient African teachings to celebrate children and community*. Novato, CA: New World Library.

Tedla, E. (1995). *Sankofa: African thought and education*. New York, NY: Peter Lang.

Thompson, G. L. (2002). *Afrikan American teens discuss their schooling experiences*. Westport, CT: Bergin & Garvey.

Watson, C., & Smitherman, G. (1996). *Educating African American males: Detroit's Malcolm X Academy solution*. Chicago, IL: Third World Press.

Williams, J. K. (2011, October). The language of Adinkra. *New York Amsterdam News*. Retrieved from http://search.proquest.com/docview/903554512?accountid=14584

Wilson, A. (1998). *Blueprint for Black Power: A moral, political, and economic imperative for the Twenty-first century*. New York, NY: Afrikan World InfoSystems.

INDEX

B

baba, 9, 28, 56, 72
Baba Shombay, 56, 72, 73, 75
Ballantine, J. H. & Hammack, F. M.,
    24, 152
Banks, J. A., 21, 152
Bishop Henry McNeal Turner, 14
Black consciousness, 8
Black Nationalism, 7, 12, 13, 14, 15, 28,
    100, 133
Black Power, 14, 15, 16, 19, 27, 28, 39,
    62, 134
Black Student Union, 111, 118
Black Studies, 15, 20, 66
Black Value System, 23
Brady, J. E., & Prufer, K. M., 67, 152
Broadside Press, 81
Brown vs. Board of Education
    legislation, 26

C

Carnoy, M., 24, 140, 152
Chancellor Williams, 80
charter schools, 25, 26, 29, 30, 31, 32,
    34, 39
Civil Rights Movements, 14
Clarke, J. H., 67
Cline, A., 141, 152
Coelho & Clarke, 1, 3, 4, 13, 17, 19, 26,
    33, 37, 39, 42, 48, 55, 76, 117, 127,
    145, 147
cognitive styles, 24
confraternity of the Brotherhood, 11
Council of Independent Black Institutions
    (CIBI), 25, 40, 44, 45, 49, 76, 77, 82,
    98, 103, 106, 123, 128, 146
cultural awareness, 4
cultural pride, 10
cultural reclamation, 10, 72, 136, 147
culturally relevant, 28, 31, 138, 142

D

Darling-Hammond, L, 31, 154
Datnow, A., & Cooper, R., 143, 152
desegregation, 27, 31
Detroit, Michigan, 30, 31
diaspora, 9, 14, 16, 29, 39, 46, 47, 79, 80,
    81, 85, 110, 138
discrimination, 4, 6
dominant paradigm, 21
Doughty, J. J., 27, 28, 29, 152
Dream, 1, 2, 3, 4, 5, 36, 37, 42, 145
DuBois, W. E. B., 64

E

Elijah Muhammad, 6, 7, 8, 9, 14
Ennis, R. H., 95, 152
Essien-Udom, E. U., 13, 14, 152
Eurocentric, 16, 21, 22, 24, 25, 95, 96, 131,
    132, 137, 141
European colonialism, 14

F

Faizah Shule Academy for Gifted Children,
    34, 40, 41, 43, 44, 45, 60, 61, 62, 64,
    69, 92, 98, 123
Fard Muhammad, 7, 9
Father Knows Best, 5
Freedom City, 39, 41, 42, 60, 61, 63, 64, 67,
    73, 75
Freire, P., 140
Frogmore, South Carolina, 28
Fruit of Islam, 8, 10

G

Geertsen, H. R., 96, 153
Gibbs, J., 141, 153

Mumbi, 56, 72, 73, 74, 81, 101, 114, 127
Mungazi, D. A., 82, 83, 154
Murrell Jr., P. C., 22, 30, 31, 34, 154
Muslim Girls Training and General
    Civilization Class, 7
Mwalimu, 46, 48, 52, 96
Mwanafunzi, 37, 46

N

Naimah, 56, 62, 63, 64, 78, 79, 83, 85, 86,
    87, 89, 94, 97, 98, 106, 107, 108, 111,
    118, 119, 120, 122, 123, 132, 133, 134
narratives, 36, 53, 56, 79, 103, 129
Nat Turner School, 39, 40
nation building, 21, 25, 28, 29, 44, 74, 78,
    79, 80, 81, 82, 85, 87, 94, 97, 100,
    110, 124, 127, 128, 129, 133, 136,
    141, 143, 146
Nation of Islam, 6, 7, 8, 9, 12, 17
nationalists, 7, 14, 16, 17, 19, 24, 28, 39, 58,
    62, 69, 70, 77, 87, 134, 141
Nelson Mandela, 98
Nguzo Saba, 23, 28, 29, 47, 52, 53, 84, 98,
    110, 111, 112, 113, 114, 116, 129, 132
Nia, 23, 98
Niger Valley, 14
Nile Valley Learning Circle, 41, 48, 50, 51
Nina, 56, 68, 70, 73, 83, 91, 93, 94, 96, 107,
    109, 110, 113, 115, 116, 121, 122, 130,
    131
No Child Left Behind legislation, 30
Nobles, W. W., 20, 154

O

Ocean Hill-Brownsville, 27
Ochs, E., & Capps, L., 36, 154
Okafor, V. O., 15, 154
Orfield, G., Eaton, S. E., & Harvard Project
    on School Desegregation., 31, 154

P

Pan Africanism, 28
Paul Cuffe, 14
Permutt, P., 67, 154
Pollard, D. S., & Ajirotutu, C. S., 31, 34,
    35, 154
principle of favorability, 33, 34
Pyramid Learning Circle, 41, 48, 50, 52
Pyramid Performance Troupe, 99

R

racial solidarity, 7
racialization, 11
racism, 4, 6, 15, 16, 26, 142
Rashid, H. M. & Muhammad, Z., 9, 154
Ratteray, J. D., & Shujaa, M. J., 27, 155
Ravitch, D., 16, 155
Redkey, E. S., 14, 155
Revolutionary Pan-African Nationalism,
    28, 29
rites of passage, 86, 90, 99, 101, 102, 105,
    106, 107, 108, 109, 110, 114, 118, 120,
    123, 124, 125, 129, 130, 132
Robinson, C. L., 15, 155
Rockquemore, K., 30, 155

S

Salaam, A., 7, 8, 155
Sankofan education, 46
Santiago, 3, 33, 34, 36, 77, 117, 145, 147,
    148
Saturday schools, 28
Schlesinger Jr., A. M., 16, 155
scholars, 12, 22, 23, 25, 40, 46, 73, 92, 103
self-determination, 7, 12, 14, 16, 17, 22, 23,
    29, 36, 46, 47, 49, 73, 87, 89, 94, 100
self-efficacy, 5, 17
self-love, 7, 8

ROCHELLE BROCK &
RICHARD GREGGORY JOHNSON III,
Executive Editors

Black Studies and Critical Thinking is an interdisciplinary series which examines the intellectual traditions of and cultural contributions made by people of African descent throughout the world. Whether it is in literature, art, music, science, or academics, these contributions are vast and far-reaching. As we work to stretch the boundaries of knowledge and understanding of issues critical to the Black experience, this series offers a unique opportunity to study the social, economic, and political forces that have shaped the historic experience of Black America, and that continue to determine our future. Black Studies and Critical Thinking is positioned at the forefront of research on the Black experience, and is the source for dynamic, innovative, and creative exploration of the most vital issues facing African Americans. The series invites contributions from all disciplines but is specially suited for cultural studies, anthropology, history, sociology, literature, art, and music.

Subjects of interest include (but are not limited to):

- EDUCATION
- SOCIOLOGY
- HISTORY
- MEDIA/COMMUNICATION
- RELIGION/THEOLOGY
- WOMEN'S STUDIES

- POLICY STUDIES
- ADVERTISING
- AFRICAN AMERICAN STUDIES
- POLITICAL SCIENCE
- LGBT STUDIES

For additional information about this series or for the submission of manuscripts, please contact Dr. Brock (Indiana University Northwest) at brock2@iun.edu or Dr. Johnson (University of San Francisco) at rgjohnsoniii@usfca.edu.

To order other books in this series, please contact our Customer Service Department:

(800) 770-LANG (within the U.S.)
(212) 647-7706 (outside the U.S.)
(212) 647-7707 FAX

Or browse online by series at www.peterlang.com.